"Keats - The Progress of the Odes. Unity and Utopia."

BREMER BEITRÄGE ZUR LITERATUR- UND IDEOLOGIEGESCHICHTE

Herausgegeben von
Thomas Metscher und Dieter Herms

Band 6

Verlag Peter Lang
Frankfurt am Main · Bern · New York · Paris

Jennifer Farrell

»Keats – The Progress of the Odes. Unity and Utopia.«

Verlag Peter Lang
Frankfurt am Main · Bern · New York · Paris

CIP-Titelaufnahme der Deutschen Bibliothek

Farrell, Jennifer:

Keats - the progress of the odes, unity and utopia / Jennifer Farrell. - Frankfurt am Main ; Bern ; New York ; Paris : Lang, 1989
  (Bremer Beiträge zur Literatur- und Ideologiegeschichte ; Bd. 6)
  ISBN 3-631-40819-6

NE: GT

Typeset by The Copy Bureau, Galway, Ireland

ISSN 0176-5205
ISBN 3-631-40819-6
© Verlag Peter Lang GmbH, Frankfurt am Main 1989
All rights reserved.

All parts of this publication are protected by copyright. Any utilisation outside the strict limits of the copyright law, without the permission of the publisher, is forbidden and liable to prosecution. This applies in particular to reproductions, translations, microfilming, and storage and processing in electronic retrieval systems.

dedicated to

Renate *and* **Jack Mitchell**

CONTENTS

Introduction 9

Ode to Psyche 10

Ode to a Nightingale 26

Ode on a Grecian Urn 54

Ode on Melancholy 75

To Autumn 88

Conclusions 101

INTRODUCTION

Why yet another book on Keats? It was Hegel that said the familiar is not necessarily recognised merely because it is familiar.[1] Keats' *"Beauty is truth, truth beauty"*, is certainly familiar but has its meaning really been recognised? While working on an interpretation of the odes of spring and autumn 1819 I discovered that the real meaning of the enigmatic aphorism and the unifying meanings and preoccupations of the ode sequence as a whole are mutually conditioning. Each, in a special sense, is the key to the other. What emerged was a new reading of these poems differing radically from the widespread view expressed, for instance, by G. S. Fraser:

The basic theme of the odes, the tension between our painful sense of transience and our intuitions of the eternal, (...) is a central theme of modern poetry.[2]

This would seem to make Keats a forerunner of the 'modernist' trend in modern poetry. Close analysis indicated otherwise. I found embodied in the odes a crucial struggle around two main, interconnected problems: the true nature of beauty and the relationship between art, artist and life. Related issues such as the sequence in which the odes were written and a contrast of poetry and sculptured art, culminating in a defence of poetry, are embedded in the developing themes of the odes. In my analyses of the odes I hope to show that the outcome of their debate would appear to underline that Keats deserves his place alongside Shelley and Byron as one of those who have been called the revolutionary Romantics.

ODE TO PSYCHE

*"However it may be, O for Life of
Sensations rather than of Thoughts!"*

November 1817

Ode to Psyche was almost certainly the first written of the sequence of great odes that is the subject of this book. H. W. Garrod has provided considerable evidence for this, where he shows the part played by **Pysche** in Keats' development of the sonnet form into the basic stanza of the odes.³ This poem stands somewhat apart from the train of thought connecting the other odes. Its themes are: the poet's vocation as priest of the human soul, the quality of poetry necessary to fulfil this task and the relationship between poetry and thought. For Keats this means a transition from 'purely' sensuous poetry to a kind that makes a conscious effort to cross-fertilise the fruits of the imagination and those of the *"working brain"*.

Psyche, the goddess of the human soul, was initially a human being. She only entered the Olympian scene with Apuleius' tale in **The Golden Ass**, thus coming too late for pagan worship. This tale ends with her elevation to immortality after marrying Cupid at the end of a long series of trials.

Keats' opening *"O Goddess!"* indicates that the ode begins where the legend leaves off:

*O Goddess! hear these tuneless numbers, wrung
By sweet enforcement and remembrance dear,
And pardon that thy secrets should be sung
Even into thine own soft-conched ear:*

ODE TO PSYCHE

It is the poet's nature as an artist that forces him to overcome his feeling of inadequacy and relate what he has seen. *"Thy secrets"* renews the thought that what the poet is about to reveal has not been recorded by mythology. Already by the end of the line, however, the previous sense of not doing justice to the deity experiences modification: *"sung"* is incompatible with *"tuneless"* and *"wrung"*. Singing, as the most intense form of vocal expression, seems the appropriate approach to a goddess, and accordingly Psyche's *"soft-conched ear"* is the most vivid image in the introduction. Already the poet is **acting** as the deity's priest.

The introduction is followed by a question indicating uncertainty as to whether the poet was asleep or awake when he beheld the vision - a lack of certainty that often seems conducive to artistic creativity in Keats:[4]

>*Surely I dreamt to-day, or did I see*
>*The winged Psyche with awaken'd eyes?*

This hint at poetic inspiration is deepened in:

>*I wander'd in a forest thoughtlessly,*

Absence of what Keats termed *"consecutive reasoning"* [5] is the hallmark of his early writing where he relies predominantly on the intuitive imagination to arrive at truth.[6] With this in mind it becomes clear that the vision about to be described will be expressed in sensuous, 'unreflecting' poetry.

Two insertions cut into the rhythmic flow of the line and so contribute to the feeling of astonishment:

>*And, on the sudden, fainting with surprise,*

This is followed by a vivid description of the scene:

>*Saw two fair creatures, couched side by side*
>*In deepest grass, beneath the whisp'ring roof*

> *Of leaves and trembled blossoms, where there ran*
> *A brooklet, scarce espied:*

The image radiates sensuous luxury and perfect tranquility. The change from the startled amazement expressed in the line before makes itself felt in the regular flowing rhythm. The image of an Eden-like retreat is constructed carefully around the lovers. Apart from softness and coolness, the grass provides protection from discovery. Nature shields the gods from all sides. There is a contradiction, characteristic of Keats' imagery, between *"whisp'ring"* and *"trembled"*, implying arrested movement inside a greater movement. Balancing on the verge of the conventional 'trembling blossoms' Keats makes the reader more perceptive to the dynamism of his image. The sensory complexity of the overall image is increased by *"brooklet"* with its associations of coolness, motion and faint sound. *"Scarce espied"* not only links up with this diminutive form but also suggests that hardly anybody has strayed into this bower of the gods.

The idyllic harmony and beauty of this natural paradise brings to mind the poetic woodlands of Milton and Shakespeare. Keats' vision of Psyche and Cupid is embedded in this literary background. The poetry of this forest becomes the forest of poetry. In turn the forest of poetry induces this vision, the poetry of this ode.

Now the view closes in:

> *'Mid hush'd, cool-rooted flowers, fragrant-eyed,*
> *Blue, silver-white, and budded Tyrian,*   (lines 14-15)

"Hush'd" continues the contradictory impression of faint sound and quietness. The attributes that follow appeal to the thermal and olfactory senses deepening the multisensory build-up of the image, and then brilliant colour bursts in. This sudden intensity of colour is enhanced through shifting the stress on to the first syllable. The succession of three stresses in the transition from line 14 to line 15 helps convey the idea of a cluster of flowers. This is deepened by the density of the 'bunched' pieces of different information given. While *"Blue"* is not

very specific, the ensuing colours become increasingly so. *"Silver-white"* complements *"Blue"* in its suggestion of coolness. *"Tyrian"* clashes with this. This latter colour has passionate associations in direct opposition to the foregoing tranquility, paralleling the tension between the poet's excitement at his discovery and the peaceful quiet he encounters. The suggestion of energy contained in *"Tyrian"*, heightened by *"budded"*, indicates the physical and emotional nature of the gods' love. The recurrent use of the past participle creates the impression that nature is holding its breath, as it were, so as not to disturb the sleep of these gods. At the same time nature does not come to a complete standstill. There is a complex background of slight movement and sound - nature's life is going on, even if at a more cautious pace.

This impression is extended into the following image *"They lay calm-breathing on the bedded grass"*. The harmony, even conspiracy, between nature and the gods is intensified: nature has made the bed for Psyche and Cupid.

The poet's attention is turned directly to the couple, described only indirectly up until now:

> *They lay calm-breathing on the bedded grass;*
> *Their arms embraced, and their pinions too;*
> *Their lips touch'd not, but had not bade adieu,*
> *As if disjoined by soft-handed slumber,*
> *And ready still past kisses to outnumber*
> *At tender eye-dawn of aurorean love:*

The loving of Psyche and Cupid - epitomising love among the pagan gods - is presented as something natural, because sensual. This heightens their physical presence, their complete integration into nature. The half-kiss brings the gods into a kind of tension identical to that of their environment. Once again nature - this time in the shape of sleep personified - is in conspiracy with the gods. The tenderness and delicacy with which they are treated (*"soft-handed"*) expresses this. The sensuality of their love is underlined by the anticipation of further kisses. *"At tender eye-dawn of aurorean love"* once more highlights, in the contradictory image of the blaze and coolness of sunrise, this fusion of passion and tranquility. At the same time the image renews the poet's celebration of Psyche's victory over Venus and her successful fight for Cupid, her right to see Cupid in the light. Therefore the stress on *"eye-dawn"* refers to more than just their awakening; it implies that Cupid no longer disappears before the break of day and above all that this is now the true dawn of their love.

The poet's esteem for the strength of Psyche's love and her defiance of Venus' tyranny is reiterated in the final

> *The winged boy I knew;*
> *But who wast thou, O happy, happy dove?*
> *His Psyche **true**!*
>
> (my emphasis, JF)

Compared to the other odes - with the possible exception of **Ode on Melancholy** - there has been relatively little written on **Ode to Psyche.**

Sometimes the relationship between body and spirit is seen as the key to an understanding of this ode. Thus Mayhead writes about the poet's vision in stanza I:

> *The union of Eros and Psyche thus strikes one as being sensual and pure at the same time.* [7]

Mayhead sees Psyche as representing spiritual values, Cupid as embodying physical love:

> *This is what has come to the poet with the force of a revelation. Sexual love and spiritual values are no longer seen as incompatible, as though one had to be shame-faced about the first in presence of the other.* [8]

Leaving aside the Christian view inherent in Mayhead's approach here which he superimposes on Keats, a closer look at the text reveals that it is the **physical** nature of Psyche's love which is at the centre of attention. In the very ideality of this physical love and physical beauty lies the only spiritual quality. It is only later on in the ode that Psyche's significance as soul gains importance while preserving her corporeality. The simultaneous presence of spirit and body is thus in Phyche herself. **She** has a 'double' nature. Her physicality is idealised, her ideality takes the shape of perfect physical beauty. This finds a parallel in the natural surroundings. Their ideal beauty contains nothing that nature does not provide. It is the kind of perfection of the natural world that one so often encounters in Keats.

Kenneth Allott [9] and others have pointed out the importance of Keats' theory of the world as *"vale of Soul-making"* [10] in understanding the poet's concept of Psyche. Keats developed this theory polemically as an alternative to the Christian tenet of the world as a vale of tears. The theory is based on the assumption that particles endowed with intelligence come into the world and are there formed into souls through the fusion of spirit (*"intelligence"* / *"Mind"*) and body (*"human heart"*) in a world *"where the heart must feel and suffer in a thousand diverse ways"*.[11] The soul is thus seen as an indivisible unity of body and spirit in contrast to the Christian view of the soul as something exclusively spiritual, which determines some critics' understanding of Psyche.

II

In his renewed address to Psyche in stanza II the poet extols her special qualities: her belated introduction into mythology, and her beauty - the beauty of a human being which once rivalled and now exceeds that of the goddess Venus. Psyche's exclusion from pagan worship and her physical splendour become the theme of stanzas II and III:

O latest born and loveliest vision far
Of all Olympus' faded hierarchy!

Her beauty alone seems to give Psyche the right to succeed the "faded hierarchy" and she now takes over from the Olympians as they once did from the Titans. This law of history had been expounded by Oceanus:

> 'As Heaven and Earth are fairer, fairer far
> 'Than Chaos and blank Darkness, though once chiefs;
> 'And as we show beyond that Heaven and Earth
> 'In form and shape compact and beautiful,
> 'In will, in action free, companionship,
> 'And thousand other signs of purer life;
> 'So on our heels a fresh perfection treads,
> 'A power more strong in beauty, born of us
> 'And fated to excel us, as we pass
> 'In glory that old Darkness: nor are we
> 'Thereby more conquer'd, than by us the rule
> 'Of shapeless Chaos. Say, doth the dull soil
> 'Quarrel with the proud forests it hath fed,
> 'And feedeth still, more comely than itself?
> 'Can it deny the chiefdom of green groves?
> 'Or shall the tree be envious of the dove
> 'Because it cooeth, and hath snowy wings
> 'To wander wherewithal and find its joys?
> 'We are such forest-trees, and our fair boughs
> 'Have bred forth, not pale solitary doves,
> 'But eagles golden-feather'd, who do tower
> 'Above us in their beauty, and must reign
> 'In right thereof; for 'tis the eternal law
> 'That first in beauty should be first in might:
> 'Yea, by that law, another race may drive
> 'Our conquerors to mourn as we do now. [12]

In contrast to the Christian concept of the pagan gods being replaced by Christ - expressed for example in Milton's **On the Morn of Christ's Nativity** - the Christian age is simply eliminated from Keats' genealogy. Not Christ but Psyche is the new power, more strong in beauty, the only true human among the Olympian gods.

ODE TO PSYCHE

Following this confrontation with the entirety of the Olympians Psyche's splendour is contrasted with that of the two goddesses especially renowned for their loveliness:

> *Fairer than Phoebe's sapphire-region'd star,*
> *Or Vesper, amorous glow-worm of the sky;*

Phoebe is still very attractive and precious, placed in the translucent dark blue of the night sky. Nonetheless, her beauty is cold and her corporeality reduced to that of a **celestial** body. Venus lacks even this dignity, being almost ridiculed in *"amorous glow-worm"*.

From this celebration of Psyche's beauty the poet turns his attention to the pagan ritual of worship which she missed because of her late advent:

> *Fairer than these, though temple thou hast none,*
> *Nor altar heap'd with flowers;*
> *Nor virgin-choir to make delicious moan*
> *Upon the midnight hours;*
> *No voice, no lute, no pipe, no incense sweet*
> *From chain-swung censer teeming;*
> *No shrine, no grove, no oracle, no heat*
> *Of pale-mouth'd prophet dreaming.*

The poet's evocation of pagan ritual is vivid. Controlled rhythmic variation brings it back to life for the moment. Counterposed to the attraction of this ritual, Psyche's magnificence is enhanced. The images of what is denied appeal to different senses in succession. First there is a heightening of the visual. Exquisite sound is added in the image of the virgin-choir. The drawing out of this *"delicious moan"* over several *"midnight hours"* is reinforced by the run-on line. From the choir-music the poet moves on to a single voice. The attention then shifts to string and wind instruments, thus creating a highly complex acoustic image. There is a rhythmic contrast between the legato of the choir image and the staccato of the series of monosyllables following it. This rhythmic contrast is repeated in the last three lines of the stanza.

"Incense sweet" introduces the sense of smell to the image. In *"From chain-swung censer teeming"* the feeling of slow swinging is rhythmically expressed in the deliberateness of the three successive stressed syllables, which changes to an alternating of stressed and unstressed syllables in the second half of the line. This movement from heavy to-and-fro to a lighter rhythm corresponds to the change in attention from the heavy metal censer, hanging by its chains, to the incense rising lightly from it. The same rhythmic pattern is used in the stanza's final line to convey the eerie sensation of prophetic trance.

Certain similarities between this section of the ode and some lines from Milton's **On the Morn of Christ's Nativity** have been pointed out.[13] The echoes show how much 'standard equipment' Keats used in these lines and yet they are not derivative and come alive in the reader's imagination - despite the added difficulty of an 11-fold negation - intensifying Psyche's splendour and the poet's wish to become her priest.

III

The second and the third stanzas are closely connected in their structure and movement. *"O brightest"* re-emphasises Psyche's supreme living quality. The reference to antiquity, the worship of old, becomes less evocative here:

> *O brightest! though too late for antique vows,*
> *Too, too late for the fond believing lyre,*
> *When holy were the haunted forest boughs,*
> *Holy the air, the water, and the fire;*

The poet's greater emotional distance, his almost laconic reference to those days shows he does not wish them back, but accepts the fact that they are past and done. What has remained is paganism, without hierarchy and formality, in the poet's attitude to the human soul. (Compare this with Wordsworth's attitude expressed in **The World Is Too Much With Us,** where times past are considered holy when people were at one with nature. This is held up against the contemporary world. Keats, however, acts as a pagan in his own time, creating a pagan relationship between himself and Psyche.)

The following lines move from 'those days' to *"these days"* :

> *Yet even in these days so far retir'd*
> *From happy pieties, thy lucent fans,*
> *Fluttering among the faint Olympians,*
> *I see, and sing, by my own eyes inspir'd.*

"Pieties", which in the context of Keats' attitude to Christianity has an almost negative connotation, is modified by *"happy"*. *"Happy"* sets these pieties against the Christian ones.

The image of Psyche, hinting at her traditional depiction as a butterfly, is the most vivid image in the first half of the stanza. The fluttering Psyche is the only thing moving among the otherwise *"faint Olympians"*, faint both in colour and strength.

The poet's wish to replace all pagan ritual with his art suggests the magnitude of his undertaking and also the true function of poetry. According to this concept poetry is to take over completely from religion in serving the needs of the human soul; poetry is seen as the appropriate form of 'worship' while religion is outmoded:

> *So let me be thy choir, and make a moan*
> *Upon the midnight hours;*
> *Thy voice, thy lute, thy pipe, thy incense sweet*
> *From swinged censer teeming;*
> *Thy shrine, thy grove, thy oracle, thy heat*
> *Of pale-mouth'd prophet dreaming.*

The emphasis is on *"me"*. In spite of the general similarity to the previous stanza some changes should not pass unnoticed. Both *"temple"* and *"altar"* are eliminated, as they will play an important part in the final stanza. The image of the censer has been changed: the censer's movement is arrested while the teeming of incense continues, infusing the image with more contained dynamism.

IV

The final stanza opens with even greater resolution: *"I will be"* replaces *"let me be"* and the poet now visualises constructive activity. He will not merely copy and repeat, but become creatively active. He will build a temple of his own:

> *Yes, I will be thy priest, and build a fane*
> *In some untrodden region of my mind,*

The more abstract term *"fane"* indicates what is to become clear in the next line: the location of the temple in the **mind**. The mind is described in sensuous terms. *"Untrodden region"* brings back stanza I and the area in which the gods were discovered. In both stanzas the image is of an unexplored part of a forest. However, stanza IV is not a simple reproduction of the first stanza. Its fusion of the spiritual and the physical is on a different level. Its vivid, sensuous images are closely linked to the mind. There is no question here of 'thoughtlessly' creating poetry:

> *Where branched thoughts, new grown with pleasant pain,*
> *Instead of pines shall murmur in the wind:*

The juxtaposition of *"branched"* and *"pines"* is interesting. The thoughts are to branch out like the *"whisp'ring roof"* of stanza I. This kind of thinking is to replace the more isolated, unconnected pine-thoughts. The image suggests a deciduous tree and this is particularly apt for the brain, as it corresponds more truly to its actual shape and appearance than a pine. It is behind images such as this that one senses Keats' medical training: branched out thoughts are proper to the brain while pine-thoughts do not do it justice.

The following lines expand on the area covered by these thought-branches:

> *Far, far around shall those dark-cluster'd trees*
> *Fledge the wild-ridged mountains steep by steep;*

This suggests enormous expanses of plains and heights. *"Dark-cluster'd"* implies density of growth, the intertwining of these thoughts. *"Fledge"* is a typical Keatsianism: it suggests simultaneously mountain edges and ledges as well as their being covered by a blanket of new, interweaving branches. There is a similar tension between *"Fledge"* and *"wild-ridged"*. Lines 7-14 develop the allusion to stanza I:

> *And there by zephyrs, streams, and birds, and bees,*
> *The moss-lain Dryads shall be lull'd to sleep;*
> *And in the midst of this wide quietness*
> *A rosy sanctuary will I dress*
> *With the wreath'd trellis of a working brain,*
> *With buds, and bells, and stars without a name,*
> *With all the gardener Fancy e'er could feign,*
> *Who breeding flowers, will never breed the same:*

The characteristically multisensory image is once more one of complete harmony between nature and its creatures in pleasant spring/summer climate. The mind's eye moves away from the wooded hills to the area they surround. It is here in the secluded centre of the fane that the poet wants to build a *"sanctuary"*. The sanctuary is dressed with flowers as was the altar in ancient times. But these flowers are different. They appear as natural as those on the pagan altar, but they are produced by the marriage of *"Fancy"* and the *"working brain"*. Interestingly, the *"working brain"* provides the hold, the *"trellis"*, for the products of Fancy. *"Dress"*, like *"build"* before, implies the poet's active endeavour. *"Wreath'd trellis"* again conjures up the brain's anatomical appearance.

The fact that fancy, like nature, never breeds identical flowers suggests its creativity, which in its turn stimulates the brain's unceasing productivity. Far from being an obstacle to fancy, the brain serves as a hold for its ever new flowers. The blossoms' unfamiliarity and therefore anonymity renews the close links between this image and that of the opening stanza.

In contrast to the enclosed bower of stanza I, however, ranging vistas are brought into view here. This intellectual region is not only larger but also richer in resources than the restricted and 'purely' sensuous bower of stanza I:

*And there shall be for thee all soft delight
That shadowy thought can win,
A bright torch, and a casement ope at night,
To let the warm Love in!*

Psyche's foreseen delight in this sanctuary within a new, unexplored region of the poet's mind is expressed in sensual, not spiritual terms. In this final image Keats reasserts his partisanship for Psyche by providing a blazing torch for her rather than the feeble oil lamp through which she had once incurred the wrath of the gods. The image demonstrates that the new type of thought-poetry is to take up the sensuousness of the earlier poetry and reproduce it at a higher level.

This synthesis, rather than being detrimental to art, in fact enhances it. The brain and the imagination work and develop in dialectical interrelation. Thought is not imposed from the outside, crippling the productivity and fertility of the imaginative faculty, but instead arises from it and stimulates it. The implications are of a new quality of poetry and of a new level of thought. Thought is not seen as a fetter to the poetic comprehension of the material world's totality, instead, it grows out of artistic insight and assists it. This form of thought in its openendedness is essentially different from the kind Keats sometimes attacked in his letters for its 'closed' nature which could never arrive at truth.[14] As *"shadowy"* implies, however, these thoughts are not yet clear and seizable. Once this new quality of poetry is achieved, the poet will be able to fulfil his true function as the priest of Psyche, the human soul.

On the whole, critics agree that **Ode to Psyche** deals with the creative process and the function of the poet. Thus Mayhead writes:

ODE TO PSYCHE

> *Attentive reading of the **Ode to Psyche** shows that one main theme of the poem is the nature of poetic composition itself. It is the only one of the odes in which Keats writes of himself as a practising artist.*[15]

There is, however, more disagreement among critics than agreement. I should like to dwell for a moment upon the former in order to highlight certain tendencies in criticism that will gain in prominence when we discuss the other odes.

Allott and Perkins interpret the vision of stanza I as a paradise which is irreconcilably opposed to the *"actual world"*,[16] the *"world of process"*.[17] At the heart of these and other interpretations lies the imposition of the critic's own disenchantment with the contemporary world, often coupled with a profound fear of thought. This is felt, for example, in the following remarks:

> *(...) the March of Mind has upset the balance of our natures, making the simple enjoyment of an experience in an 'eternal moment' an almost heroic achievement. Keats's regret embraces his own loss of an earlier innocence.*[18]

But Keats says the very opposite of this! The ode's theme is the necessity of a new kind of poetry emerging from the marriage of the imagination with thought - if the poet is to fulfil his obligation to the human soul. This transition from the old to the new quality of verse is enacted in the ode.

Part of the reason for some critics' reversal of the poem's real theme seems to lie in the increasingly widespread desire to rope Keats into the camp of those Romantics who turned their back on actuality. This desire would seem to emerge, for instance, from the following comment by Perkins:

> *(.....) the visionary and the mortal cannot be known simultaneously or in juxtaposition (....) the poet must*

> *protectively isolate the vision in order to enjoy it. To the extent that he consecrates his own mind as a "shrine" to Psyche he retreats from confronting "the agonies, the strife/ Of human hearts"* [19]

And Allott writes in a similar vein:

> *(...) Keats will be able to preserve the visionary poetic experience from marauding analysis (...)* [20]

If the poet seriously wanted to retreat from human concerns, why then should he make the human soul his goddess? Moreover, the involvement of thought processes in creating a poetry in service of Psyche indicates that the poet feels the necessity to face the more immediate requirements of humanity. The important role attributed to thought as the hold for fancy's products is - to put it mildly - misrepresented in *"marauding analysis"*. Allott places himself on a par with Wordsworth who comes to a similar estimation of analytical thinking and the striving for knowledge in **The Excursion.**[21] In **Ode to Psyche**, however, no such pessimistic and negative view of the advance of knowldege and thought is put forward, in fact the opposite emerges: by contrasting the vistaless bower of stanza I with the open expanse of stanza IV the poet demonstrates the endless creativity and potential of cross-fertilising creative thought and imagination.

Stuart M. Sperry, the American critic, shares the basic trend of this criticism, embellishing it with a certain philosophical pretentiousness. The critic's intention is to make Keats voice *"the necessity of a new kind of poetry (....) of an increasing inwardness and subjectivity"*.[22] Thus Sperry cuts Keats to conform with the world as he and fellow-spirits perceive it:

> *Indeed the recognition the ode finally intimates is that for the poet of the present day there can be no escape from shadowiness and subjectivity, that the effort to push further into the region of the unknown leads only to the perception*

ODE TO PSYCHE

> *of further passages and implications, that it results in a sense of ultimate inconclusiveness that is ironic.*[23]

It is bewildering how Sperry can read the final stanza as being pessimistic regarding cognition and life. The images of the *"wide quietness"* and the *"sanctuary"* contain no threat or even hint of darkness! On the contrary, dryads are "lull'd to sleep" - nature is in complete harmony with itself and the creatures it houses. All these images are swept under the carpet to serve a purpose alien to Keats. Those readers, however, who approach the poem with an open mind and let it speak for itself will take from the **Ode to Psyche** a positive attitude to the role of thought in poetry - and in life - and therefore to the cognisability and changeability of the world.

ODE TO A NIGHTINGALE

To be, or not to be: that is the question:
Whether 'tis nobler in the mind to suffer
The slings and arrows of outrageous fortune,
Or to take arms against a sea of troubles,
And by opposing end them?

Hamlet's question lies at the heart of **Ode to a Nightingale**, constituting its universal and, as it were, timeless appeal. The meaning of life is not something unchanging, but any serious struggle for an answer in a particular epoch must remain significant for generations to come. Life has its underlying continuity after all, and Hamlet's question is as relevant in our own time as it was in Keats' day.

Within this general question, however, Keats posed another, which affected the Romantics in a very specific sense. What this is, is perhaps best understood by comparing the first generation of Romantics with the second. At the time when **Ode to a Nightingale** was written, Wordsworth, Coleridge and Southey had drawn in their revolutionary horns and were already being regarded by their successors as the kind of traitor that Browning was to describe. Keats' ode and the one following it - **Ode on a Grecian Urn** - show how the poet was torn between the attraction of escaping from the world or facing it through art. The lyrical subject in these two odes lives through a crucial struggle and this helps to determine the greatness and relevance of the poetry. **Ode to a Nightingale** and **Ode on a Grecian Urn** form a separate group within the cycle of odes in that they embody the poet's progressing artistic search for a valid concept of beauty. The concept arising out of this struggle underlies the kind of melancholy celebrated in **Ode on Melancholy** and is the major theme of **To Autumn**.

Because of the nature of **Ode to a Nightingale** and **Ode on a Grecian Urn** as poems of fierce struggle, it is important to distinguish

- up to a point - between the poet Keats, and the 'I', which I propose to term **lyrical subject**. The distinction is important, because Keats does not - and cannot - always fully identify with the lyrical subject. Otherwise the odes would not have come down to us as coherent works of art. It will also be pointed out in the discussions of the odes that Keats always has sufficient distance from the lyrical subject to present the latter's development through the images and language employed. Nevertheless, a development within the poet Keats also takes place, though on another plane. Evidence of this is the progression within the ode sequence itself, as well as the sincerity with which Keats clearly 'lives through' the battles for a concept of true beauty. Thus, Keats and the lyrical subject should not be completely divorced from one another, but for the present purpose this differentiation is essential.

I

My heart aches, and a drowsy numbness pains
My sense, as though of hemlock I had drunk,
Or emptied some dull opiate to the drains
One minute past, and Lethe-wards had sunk:

It is out of this condition of the lyrical subject that the ode develops. By using the present tense Keats conveys the immediacy of what is felt, involving the reader directly and very personally. He does this too by opening the poem on a note of combined physical and emotional suffering (heartache) which is threatening the very existence of the lyrical subject. The almost sluggish rhythm of the opening line transmits a sense of weariness and monotony. The images however do not suggest lethargy alone. The oxymoron *"numbness pains"* creates a contradictory feeling of simultaneously deadened and alerted senses.

In explaining the reason for his plight the two lines that follow form the connecting link between the lyrical subject's portrayal of himself and his view of the nightingale:

'Tis not through envy of thy happy lot,
But being too happy in thine happiness, -

> *That thou, light-winged Dryad of the trees,*
> *In some melodious plot*
> *Of beechen green, and shadows numberless,*
> *Singest of summer in full-throated ease.*

The threefold repetition of 'happy' indicates that this freedom from cares is considered the bird's most prominent feature in contrast to the lyrical subject who projects into the bird that which he most sorely misses in his own existence. Pain, heaviness, absence of motion and colour and the nearness to death are replaced by lightness, motion, warm vitality and an abundance of vegetation. This contrast is paralleled by that between the great rhythmic variety of these lines and the monotony with which the poem opens. The oxymoron *"melodious plot"* expresses the fact that nature is at one with itself in the harmonious 'contradiction' of its parts. By singling the nightingale out of its natural surroundings the lyrical subject relates to it as the epitome of nature. The nightingale is nature's voice and - as *"Singest of summer in full-throated ease"* implies - its poet. The glimpse of the bird introduces a flash of light to which colour and movement are added in *"beechen green and shadows numberless"*. The stanza which opens with heartache ends on *"ease"*: the state the lyrical subject hopes to attain himself.

The relationship between the lyrical subject and the bird has naturally become a central issue in critical discussion of **Ode to a Nightingale**. The critic's view of what the nightingale's world actually represents already indicates the ensuing line of interpretation.

The majority of critics do not see the nightingale as a natural bird into which the lyrical subject projects the happiness he fails to find in his own life, but rather as a being transcending the mundane world. Thus the existence of two mutually exclusive worlds, the temporal and the spiritual, is postulated. The consequences of such a position have to be examined. If there are really two worlds in the poem - that of the lyrical subject and that of the nightingale - which cannot come together, then all the poem can do is to illustrate the attempt to enter the nightingale's world and its ultimate failure. Many critics would agree with this conclusion.

This interpretation strategy will emerge as the basis of a number of critical readings discussed in this and the following chapters. Perhaps one of the most extreme examples of such an approach can be found in Earl R. Wasserman's analyses in **The Finer Tone** [24]. At the heart of Wasserman's discussions of **Ode to a Nightingale** and **Ode on a Grecian Urn** lies the concept of *'heaven's bourne'* - a term which he takes from **Hymn to Pan**[25] and infuses with a meaning of his own. According to the critic *'heaven's bourne'* is

> *(...) that region where earth and the ethereal, light and darkness, time and no-time become one; (...) the outermost limit of the imagination after it has left naked the materialistic brain, which tries to seize everything in a clear, and therefore merely earthly, conception. (....) where mortal and immortal become one (...)* [26]

Naturally, as Mr Wasserman stresses several times, it is impossible for mortals *"to draw heaven and earth together into a stable union"* [27]. And since it is only at this meeting point of heaven and earth that happiness, beauty and truth exist, Keats can do little more than - after the experience of 'heaven's bourne' which the critic tells us takes place before stanza I - bemoan the fact that he is a mere mortal:

> *(.....) since "happiness" lies in the oxymoronic nature of heaven's bourne, it can be experienced only by the annihilation of self. Yet, while man is mortal the projection of self cannot be complete because the spirit cannot wholly leave behind the sensory substance in which it is encased; the effort to nourish life's self by its proper pith must torment the sensory clay.*[28]

Wasserman's 'heaven's bourne' and the human world are mutually exclusive, the former only being attainable with death. The situation of the lyrical subject at the outset of the ode has thus strong implications for the human condition. Keats, however, has implied no such separation into spirit and matter. The bird has been depicted as an integral part of nature and its realm, as it is presented in stanza I, is both natural and sensuous. These are the qualities that attract the lyrical subject. The very fact that he cannot feel at one with nature, like the bird, indicates that his life experience is a distortion of what life should be, and because he is not in concord with nature he is not at one with himself. Sensuousness and the harmony, which the lyrical subject sees between the nightingale and nature, therefore become significant factors in the kind of existence he seeks.

II

With the juxatposing of two antithetical modes of existence in stanza I as its point of departure, stanza II expresses the wish to *"fade away into the forest dim"* with the nightingale. The vehicle for this escape is to be wine. The actual expression of the wish in the final two lines of the stanza is preceded by a sensuous evocation of the wine:

> *O, for a draught of vintage! that hath been*
> *Cool'd a long age in the deep-delved earth,*
> *Tasting of Flora and the country green,*
> *Dance, and Provencal song, and sunburnt mirth!*

The word "draught" conjures up a vision of deep drinking, while in *"vintage"* the wine has matured to the quintessence of excellence. All the senses are brought into play in order to enhance the anticipated taste: the thermal (*"Cool'd"*), the tactile (*"deep-delved"*), the auditory (*"Dance"*, *"Provencal song"*, *"mirth"*), the gustatory and the visual. The visual dimension is marked by a touch of colour and motion. The warmth of the South (*"Provencal song"*) contrasts with the coolness of the wine and is intensified in *"sunburnt mirth"*. Such multisensory complexity reminiscent of the most intensely sensuous of Keats' poetry, indicates that the wine belongs to an age radically different from the one that brings about heartache. The wine's description not only appeals to the senses but brings with it a vision of a village community celebrating the harvest, of happy and carefree, singing people. The image as a whole thus serves to extend and intensify the connotations of the nightingale's world as portrayed in the opening stanza, enrichening it with a social dimension.

The subsequent sestet reasserts the longing for wine in the parallel construction *"O for a..."*, heightening the emotional intensity:

O for a beaker full of the warm South,
Full of the true, the blushful Hippocrene,
With beaded bubbles winking at the brim,
And purple-stained mouth;
That I might drink, and leave the world unseen,
And with thee fade away into the forest dim:

"Full of" indicates that abundance which is a hallmark of the nightingale's world, a world created out of the lyrical subject's longing, which is in turn born of a life experience defined by deprivation, desolation and inadequacy. The close connection between *"warm South"* and *"blushful Hippocrene"* implies that uncurtailed human life is the **true** source of poetic inspiration. As this stanza demonstrates, the lyrical subject too could sing *"of summer in full-throated ease"* if conditions were different and life what it might be.

The pull of the wine increases with the stanza's movement - from the very depths of the earth to the people upon the earth and then the approach of the beaker to the mouth. Here the sensuously concrete appeal reaches a climax: the wine itself takes an active hand in inviting the lyrical subject - *"With beaded bubbles winking at the brim"*. In the concluding image *"And purple-stained mouth"*, the wine has been imaginatively consumed and the movement within the verse finds its culmination.

Although it would appear that the last two lines of stanza II are sufficiently clear in their meaning, the significance of this verse in the ode's argument is subject to much controversy. Garrod, for example, sees no real function for them:

> *I suppose every poet takes the intoxication of his own words. The 'beechen green and shadows numberless' carry Keats' imagination to dim faraway forests into which he would gladly, 'leaving the world, unseen' fade away. But the development of the world is delayed over a whole stanza by another phrase, 'Singest of summer in full-throated ease': a phrase which dictates the immediately following (i.e. stanza II, JF)* [29]

Similarly Graham Hough makes no connection between that which oppresses the lyrical subject in his own life experience and the desired flight. Thus stanza II is interpreted as a continuation of the *"intoxication"* of stanza I:

> *the heart-ache and the drowsy numbness of the opening lines do not describe mere dejection, but a sort of drugged state, which can only be maintained by further intoxication (Stanza 2). Wine is the traditional soother of men's cares, the traditional means of prolonging a drowsy sensuous enjoyment; and Keats sometimes said he enjoyed claret.* [30]

Hough sees no conflict in stanza I between the bird's mode of being and that of the lyrical subject.[31] Indeed, he even suggests the desirability of this *"drugged state"* of the opening lines. It is, however, precisely this conflict between the two modes of existence that brings about the desire to flee with the nightingale, whose 'happiness' stimulates the vision connected with the draught of vintage. The factor which unites the world of the nightingale and that of the villagers in contrast to the one experienced by the lyrical subject is untrammelled sensuous enjoyment. So the wish to escape must be understood as a longing for richly unfolded sensuousness in an impoverished world where this is denied. This aspect will gain increasing importance in the development of the ode.

Wasserman recognises the function of stanza II as an attempt to escape, but finds that the lyrical subject fails because *"he is looking on outward forms and is negligent of spiritual values"* [32]. All images connected with the nightingale have been vividly sensuous and this-worldly, rather than spiritual and other-worldly. But this does not fit into the critic's concept of 'heaven's bourne' and so he ignores it. His intentions emerge as opposed to those of Keats.

III

Fade far away, dissolve, and quite forget
What thou among the leaves hast never known,

These opening lines intensify the desire expressed in stanza II and continue to follow the visualised movement of the bird away from its present haunt to its 'dissolution' to the eye. The main hope attached to the flight is a forgetting of the conditions of human life which oppress the lyrical subject:

3	*The weariness, the fever, and the fret*
	Here, where men sit and hear each other groan;
5	*Where palsy shakes a few, sad, last gray hairs,*
	Where youth grows pale, and spectre-thin, and dies;
7	*Where but to think is to be full of sorrow*
	And leaden-eyed despairs,
	Where Beauty cannot keep her lustrous eyes,
10	*Or new Love pine at them beyond tomorrow.*

With the word *"forget"* comes back the memory of everything that the lyrical subject wishes to erase from his mind. This sudden return to reality rather than the anticipated flight with the nightingale happens because the draught of vintage could only be imaginatively, not actually, drunk within the framework of the ode. This imagined aid to escape is clearly not sufficient.

Lines 3 to 10 depict the human condition at the beginning of the 19th century in England, as Keats experiences it (***"Here"***). But because this is such a highly generalised poetic image it can be applied to all class, exploiting society. Line 3 creates a tension which is heightened by the use of words with a decreasing number of syllables (from three to one). This culminates in the sequence of two stresses in the transition from line 3 to line 4: *"frét/Hére"*, which conveys a sense of urgency. *"Here"* is the only stressed opening of a line in this passage and thus receives particular emphasis, more so since it is followed by a caesura. This makes *"Here"* a sufficiently strong point of reference for the five ensuing relative clauses. These maintain the tension through the fivefold repetition of *"Where"*.

In the first images depicting the decay which *"Here"* encompasses from youth to old age, monosyllables and the coinciding of sense unit and line deepen the feeling of monotony and imprisonment in this condition. There is a return to the immobility, heaviness and lack of colour encountered in the opening lines of the poem. All ability to perceive sensuously is distorted - instead of music and song these people *"hear each other groan"*. There is no active communication between them. This is the pointed opposite of the world visualised in the previous stanza. Bright colours are replaced by pallor. Metrically the retardation of movement is conveyed by a sequence of five stresses[33] in the second half of line 4. While the image of old age captures an almost static condition, line 6 shows the deterioration of youth in its progression. This is the movement of death-in-life and the movement towards death itself. *"Dies"* is the 'natural' culmination of this inverted and perverted movement.

Robert Gittings expresses the widespread view held among critics that with this image of youth dying, Keats had specifically and only his youngest brother Tom in mind, who had recently died of consumption.[34] This certainly must have lent particular sharpness to the image, but in this case as all too often, the biographical element seems overemphasised to the exclusion of the more general meaning. A purely personal image would break the pattern here. The preceding and following images are of a highly generalised nature, commenting on society in its entirety. The reference to youth at this point makes clear that this is not merely a description of a sad but natural process of ageing, but is in fact an image of waste and the deterioration of life's potential.

The succeeding four lines (7 - 10) contain two images which are set apart somewhat from those just discussed. The idea expressed in lines 7 and 8 is that thought can only reflect the conditions of material existence, not 'triumph' over them. The parallel structure *"Where ..."* identifies this image with the human situation as it is depicted in the previous lines. It is under these specific historical conditions - which unfortunately also apply to other ages of class society - that thinking is sorrowful. Even though the age of the Industrial Revolution was fundamentally one of advance, a terrible price was exacted in human misery.

"Leaden-eyed despairs" is retrieved from abstraction by the sensuous adjective. This adjective also contains a twofold reference to the preceding images. First, it renews the sensations of heaviness and immobility; its combination with 'eye' reinforces the distortion of the sense-processes.

The motif of eyes is picked up again in the following line: *"Where Beauty cannot keep her lustrous eyes"*. *"Lustrous"* contains all the immense appeal of joy-in-life. The contrast effected by the direct comparison of *"leaden-eyed"* and *"lustrous eyes"*, the one alien and the other proper to healthy eyes, is deepened by the alliteration. The eyes' splendour cannot last, just as youth cannot, in this kind of environment. What is important, however is that Beauty is shown to be forever reasserting itself, as does youth. (This is partly achieved through the present tense.)

Love's short-lived pining at Beauty's eyes corresponds to the overall awareness of generations emerging and withering away without fulfilment. Here the process of renewing potential is communicated in *"new"*. Love at least displays the possibility of responding appropriately to Beauty's lustrous eyes (*"pine"*). The social environment, as it is experienced by the lyrical subject, tends to destroy Beauty and Love - concepts indicating a sensuousness proper to human existence.

Thus stanza III both embodies and relativises what is implied in stanzas I and II. It shows that the contradiction between the world as it should be and the world as it is, is not absolute. Beauty and the ability to perceive it, which is essential to human life appropriate to itself, has its source in life.

Robin Mayhead follows the majority of critics in not recognising the true nature of the nightingale's world when he writes:

> *We realize now why Keats has not been wrong in attributing his depression to 'being too happy in thine happiness'. The nightingale is imagined to be happy **because it is not human**, because it has never known 'The weariness, the fever, and the fret' of human existence. And the poet knows too well that the happiness he feels in mentally following the bird into its world 'among the leaves' cannot last, for he is a human being after all, and what is human must pass away. His depression is thus implicit in the happiness itself.* [35]

One could certainly agree with Mayhead up to a point - the bird is considered happy because of its ignorance of the human condition as it is portrayed in stanza III. Two important points should be made, however. One is that the critic takes the depiction of human existence, as Keats perceives it in his time, to represent an eternal and unchangeable human condition. Its outstanding attribute is taken to be mortality, and this is juxtaposed to the nightingale's seemingly immortal condition.

Keats, however, is not primarily concerned with human mortality but rather with the condition of death-in-life, i.e. perverted life. He is portraying two essentially different kinds of living, one that is commensurate to humanity and one that is not. The first, the nightingale's world, overcomes the distortions of Keats' experienced world. The alternative world is real nevertheless, and as stanza V will make clear, rooted in the natural growth and decline of the changing seasons. The world of nature is life as it should **and could be**.

If Keats had really seen his own world as the inevitable human condition, how then could he visualise the possibility of **human** joy-in-life as expressed in stanza II? It is precisely this tension between the potential and the actual that gives so much dynamism to the ode.

Alan Tate considers stanza III bad poetry.[36] But is it not precisely the insistence on absense of colour, motion, sensuousness which dictate its language? A close look at the text reveals how well it conveys exactly this 'message' in all its imagery. It is here at this level of artistic detail that one must search for the poem's meaning.

IV

We noted earlier that the first attempt at flight with the nightingale - through wine - didn't succeed because, though concretely imagined, it remained a secondary impression. The endeavour resulted in a vision of the 'nightingale-world', but only as an outside observer (stanza II). This led to renewed detachement from the nightingale (stanza III). In order to achieve lasting unity with the bird - and thus a successful escape - a more sustained effort in the same direction is necessary.

> *Away! away! for I will fly to thee,*
> *Not charioted by Bacchus and his pards,*
> *But on the viewless wings of Poesy.*
> *Though the dull brain perplexes and retards:*

This is a more determined effort. *"Away!"* indicates immediate and speedy flight with an urgency lacking in *"fade far away"*. Its decisiveness is heightened by the repetition of the exclamation. The positioning at the beginning of the verse effectively conveys the impression of a deliberate attempt to break away from the reflections of stanza III.

"I will fly to thee" is more resolute than *"That I **might** drink..../ And **with** thee fade away..."* The change from *"with"* to *"to"* brings greater dynamism. The distance between the lyrical subject and the bird has increased since stanzas I and II. The human world stands between them.

The ideas expressed in the first four lines of this stanza are more explicit, appear more conscious than those conveyed in the images of the earlier verses. The vehicle for escape -*"Poesy"* - is not lovingly evoked as before. The intention is clear, the determination to succeed great. As the first attempt failed, success requires that the ode itself give 'material form' to the new vehicle for escape. This means that the ode must become for the time being escape-poetry, which necessarily differs from the kind of poetry it has been up to now. The kind of poetry which is to achieve an escape from the world must exclude thought. This insight is hinted at in *"viewless wings of Poesy"*. *"Viewless"* not only refers to the invisible and light wings of the imagination in contrast to the heavy, earthy wine, or Bacchus' corpulent figure, but also points to an important quality of escape poetry: it does not see the world. (Cf. the ambiguity of *"leave the world unseen"*.) It is the brain which threatens to retard and prevent the escape, due to its unavoidable reflection of reality. The brain functioned in this way in making the lyrical subject aware of the misery surrounding him, and has further been the major factor in creating the ode itself. (On the authorial level however - as I pointed out at the beginning of this chapter - the ode as a whole is a carefully constructed **work of art** in which the 'thoughtless' poetry of stanzas IV to V plays an integral part, whereas if the poem were truly 'thoughtless' one would be faced with an incoherent effusion.)

With line 5 the lyrical subject (as 'poet') achieves the desired unity with the nightingale:

> *Already with thee!* tender is the night,
> *And haply the Queen-Moon is on her throne,*
> *Cluster'd around by all her starry Fays;*
> *But here there is no light,*
> *Save what from heaven is with the breezes blown*
> *Through verdurous glooms and winding mossy ways.*
>
> (my emphasis, JF)

In order to underline the point where the ode becomes part of the attempt to escape, i.e. where the quality of the poetry changes into 'thoughtless' verse, there is the sharpest possible caesura after reaching the nightingale. What follows contrasts strongly with anything prior to it in the ode.

As *"viewless"* anticipates, lack of sight is to be a hallmark of escape-poetry. This quality is taken up and expressed in *"tender"*, which is explicitly non-visual, though emotion-laden, whereby the tactile sense may be evoked.[37] **Perhaps** (*"haply"*) the moon is on her throne - the lyrical subject **cannot see**, because *"here there is no light"*. This fact is often overlooked by critics. Mayhead, for example, assumes that

> *(...) poetic fancy wings the poet swiftly to the nightingale in its perch up among the tree-tops, where the moon and stars can be seen (...)* [38].

Such a reading contradicts the text. The lyrical subject is clearly in the forest's darkness: *"But **here** there is no light/save ..."*. It is precisely the lack of vision that is an important key to the verse that follows. Some light is **blown** into the darkness - once again Keats makes use of a deliberately non-visual verb to express this sense-perception, which is reinforced in the alliteration of *"by the breezes blown"*. A few rays of light suffice to give spatial dimension to the forest, emerging in the last line: *"Through verdurous glooms and winding mossy ways"*. The impression is one of increasing sensory complexity, calling to mind the kind of sensuousness identified with the nightingale's world portrayed in stanzas I and II. The difference is that here the lyrical subject is no longer an outside observer but has finally entered the 'escape' world himself.

We have arrived at a stage crucial to the basic understanding of the ode. To miss this point of successful escape is a folly of some magnitude. Thus Bate, for example, writes:

> *Then, in three words, the union (i.e. of poet and bird, JF) is simply declared. But the short effort of "Poesy" - used solely in this way for escape or illusion - results only in two lines of futile ornament (the "Queen-Moon" attended by her "starry Fays").*

and further down:

> *(....) the unconvincing lines (i.e. of Poesy, JF) are followed by the admission that the poet is not really there, after all,*

but "here," in the deep twilight: (quotes lines IV, 5 - 10, JF) From now until the end of the ode the separateness of the poet and the bird is presupposed. Henceforth the poet sits and listens ("I cannot see what flowers.... Darkling I listen").[39]

Wasserman too shows himself unreceptive to the new quality of this darkness in contrast to the gloom of stanzas I and III:

(....*The night is tender with the nightingale, but it leaves the poet in blind darkness. None of the proposals, then, not even poesy, succeeds in returning the poet to empathic union with the nightingale.)*
To continue with the symbolic significance of the nightingale. With the second proposal, the bird, which had been distinguished from the mutable world, is now discovered to be in the presence of ideality. Not only is the nightingale distinct from the mutable world by never having been related to its inherent principle, decay; the night, the darkness in which the mystery resides, is tender with the nightingale, and to the bird the ideal Queen-Moon is on her throne, pouring out the light of complete illumination.[40]

Some pages on this thought is continued:

For the poet, however, there is no light into the mystery, except for the chance heaven-sent flashes lighting up the glooms and winding mossy ways that are our paths through this world of darkness.[41]

What appears to have happened is that this poetry is so convincing in its 'sensuous presence' that these (and other) critics have been deceived into taking it for a return to the initial plane of reality. It is however important to understand - as attentive reading of the text discloses - that the lyrical subject succeeds for the time being in staying with the nightingale and experiences its world. (Why else should *"fancy"* be finally rejected only in the last verse if the attempt at flight through poetry had been a feeble one extending only over two lines?) The evidence for this lies in the imagery: in the actual creation of 'viewless' poetry and in the fact that the lyrical subject himself directly perceives thriving sensuous beauty, which is the supreme quality of the Keatsian reality-tied utopia, in this case the nightingale-world. The darkness surrounding the lyrical subject is a far cry from the impoverished and alien grey world of life experienced as portrayed in stanza III. This forest is intense and intimate, nevertheless natural and with a slight, though not tenuous, connection with the outer world through the wind movement.

Mr. Wasseman, whose main method of interpretaion is assertion, painstakingly avoids any direct confrontation with the text. His comment on the second half of stanza IV is, to say the least, bizarre.

V

Stanza V continues to explore the verdurous darkness entered into in stanza IV:

> *I cannot see what flowers are at my feet,*
> *Nor what soft incense hangs upon the boughs,*
> *But, in embalmed darkness, guess each sweet*
> *Wherewith the seasonable month endows*
> *The grass, the thicket, and the fruit-tree wild;*

This forest distills the essence of all the sensuous beauty associated with the nightingale-world. Like the previous images of this utopian reality in stanzas I and II, it is made up **exclusively** of things of **this our world**. Life is the quarry for the stuff this dream is made of.

The lyrical subject is able to relate sensuously to this beauty. All his senses - except for the visual - are strained to comprehend and 'visualise' the natural surroundings. Once more he stresses *"I cannot see ..."*. But the fact that he senses the flowers at his feet turns them into a tentative visual image. A similar technique is employed in the succeeding lines, re-emphasising the non-visual, mainly olfactory, perception (*"incense"*, *"embalmed"*).

The different fragrances prompt the lyrical subject to *"guess each sweet"* and thus the visual image emerges with increasing clarity. By line 5 the image has taken on clear visual contours. On the realistic-naturalistic level the eye becomes used to the darkness as the poet walks through the forest and through the seasons. The kind of plant he comes across becomes increasingly complex. This semantic gradation is supplemented by a build-up in the number of syllables, which in its turn is complemented rhythmically: *"The grass, the thicket and the fruit-tree wild"* . The stanza continues:

> *White hawthorn, and the pastoral eglantine;*
> *Fast fading violets cover'd up in leaves;*
> *And mid-May's eldest child,*
> *The coming musk-rose, full of dewy wine,*
> *The murmurous haunt of flies on summer eves.*

Precision in visual description increases even more with the adjectives *"white"*, *"pastoral"* and *"fast fading"*. The particular combination here of violet, eglantine and musk-rose reminds one strongly of Shakespeare's

> *I know a bank where the wild thyme blows,*
> *Where oxlips and the nodding violet grows,*
> *Quite over-canopied with luscious woodbine,*
> *With sweet musk-roses and with eglantine:* [42]

This association with the forest of fancy in **A Midsummer Night's Dream** enhances the half-real, half-fantastic quality of Keats' stanza. Nature's process is introduced in the image of the violet: *"fast fading"*, *"cover'd up in leaves"*. The cycle of nature, including mutability and decay, is part of the beauty. Clearly, Keats is not upset by the **natural** process of life and death. Dying here is a natural process of life. The violet's fading is not a premature wasting away without fulfilment.

Compare this with the wasting away of human life which pains the poet and his lyrical subject: human existence under conditions alien to it (stanza III) **runs counter to** this natural cycle.

The final image is the most extensive one, embracing the remaining three lines of the stanza. The musk-rose is depicted even more strongly in its natural cycle than the violet, extending from its budding into high summer. Such an interlocking of infancy and maturity, implying endless development, is not untypical of Keats (see **To Autumn** *"full-grown lambs"*). While process concluding in death was central to the violet image, in the musk-rose, it is fulfilment. It also emphasises that organic coherence of nature as a whole, which has been a developing feature of the stanza. Here things do not exist separately, in alienation from each other. In this complex image of natural process we find the most comprehensive metaphor of what all life should and could be: this is life's true potential, the reality-tied, Keatsian utopia.

Poet and reader experience this utopia, life's humane potential, through the mental senses, and so it becomes part of their inner world like other things of beauty that

> *Haunt us till they become a cheering light*
> *Unto our souls, and bound to us so fast,*
> *That, whether there be shine, or gloom o'ercast,*
> *They always must be with us, or we die.*[43]

Art at its best strengthens our belief in human potential and the future by making it tangible. On the other hand it is only under these conditions of a 'better world' into which the lyrical subject (as poet) is integrated in stanza V that he can sing *"of summer in full-throated ease"*. To do this he must deliberately turn away from a reflection of the actual. This reveals the double-edged nature of the escape. It is successful in that the lyrical subject enters the nightingale's world by excluding the actual. It is unsuccessful in that he cannot create an unreal world but instead produces a utopia which is firmly rooted in life.

For Wasserman and other critics the lyrical subject finds himself on the cold hill-side in this stanza:

> *To read literally the poet's complaint that he cannot see the flowers would be meaningless, for not all the flowers are there to be perceived by the external senses. Were the poet able to "see" these flowers, he would, like Pan, be penetrating to nature's central principle, its full essence, and would be overcoming the temporality of the mortal world in which the inwardness of nature becomes manifest only fragmentarily. (...) But the husk of nature will not open quite to the core, and, being now only a weak mortal, the poet can only guess at this inwardness as he moves about in the darkness that surrounds all earthly existence.*[44]

Examination of the text has shown that to *"read literally the poet's complaint (?) that he cannot see the flowers"* is in fact the only way to understand his meaning. Keats is indeed "penetrating to nature's central principle", but in a way quite different from that imputed to him by Wasserman. Wasserman's concept of the material world's inscrutability contradicts the images of its real and potential transparency and cohesion.

VI

On the level of the ode's argument, unity with the nightingale has been achieved. If the poem is to continue the argument must be pushed on. This occurs with the opening of stanza VI. Its first words mark the transition back to reflection:

> *Darkling I listen; and, for many a time*
> *I have been half in love with easeful Death,*
> *Call'd him soft names in many a mused rhyme,*
> *To take into the air my quiet breath;*

The lucent forest of poetry has vanished and the lyrical subject remains in darkness. With the reintroduction of darkness a non-visual sense is once again employed: *"I listen"*. At the same time this listening is a clue to the renewed distance between the lyrical subject and the nightingale - no longer at one with the bird, he hears its song. This stanza's language is not as richly sensuous as that of the previous one. Reflection on this situation takes over from deliberately 'unreflective' description.

The thought of death is brought about by the experience of stanza V, the turning away from thought and therefore - tendentiously - from reality. A point of culmination has been reached and

Now more than ever seems it rich to die,
To cease upon the midnight with no pain,
While thou art pouring forth thy soul abroad
In such an ecstacy!

"Now" carries particular weight, indicating the emotional tension at this point where unity with the bird seems impossible to retain. *"Rich"*, the attribute of life as it could and should be, is transferred to its opposite, death. This view of death is anticipated in *"easeful"* and *"quiet breath"*. The attraction of death as a barely noticeable transition from a height of poetic achievement is the overwhelming impression of this stanza. At this point in the ode death appears as the only way left to achieve lasting unity with the bird. At the same time it marks the change to a new position taken by the lyrical subject.[45] Death seems to promise some of the nightingale-world's qualities while in fact it would put an irreversible end to all of them. Abundance of sensuous beauty and unwarped perception of it distinguish this world; the song may continue, but death cuts off its perception:

Still wouldst thou sing, and I have ears in vain -
To thy high requiem become a sod.

Here the lyrical subject realises fully what was already indicated in *"seems it rich to die"*, why once more, he has been only **half** in love with death. It is the awareness of loss of perception of the earth's beauty that makes him repudiate death as a solution.

Naturally, most discussions of this stanza centre around the problem of death. Bate, who assumes that the attempt at flight through poetry ends after two lines in stanza IV and who therefore takes the rest of that stanza and the whole of V to be a return to the actual, now writes:

> *The acceptance of process, of course, involves the acceptance of death, as the serene ode "To Autumn" especially illustrates; and while the hypnotic song of the bird continues, the thought of death, almost intolerable before ("Where youth grows pale, and spectre-thin, and dies"), now becomes "easeful".* [46]

Such an identification of the different concepts of death encountered in the ode - the harrowing condition of death-in-life in stanza III, the natural death as a condition of fulfilment in stanza V and death as the only way of lasting escape in stanza VI - is fairly current critical practice. This assumption arises logically from the false premise that Keats is concerned generally with human mortality. A distinction between the three kinds of death must be made if the ode is to be properly understood.

VII

Following the thought of the nightingale singing his requiem, the lyrical subject bursts out in a song of praise, a solemn anthem to life for the nightingale:

> *Thou wast not born for death, immortal Bird!*
> *No hungry generations tread thee down;*

This condition contrasts strongly with the lyrical subject's own experience of an existence where people are born for death, not life. Whereas in human society life is dominated by death, in that positive counter-world of nature life comes into its dominion. While the life of an individual representative of the species comes to its natural culmination as a result and condition of fulfilment, the life of nature goes on. The nightingale's immortality is also achieved through the fulfilment of its being, which the song expresses, and therefore its immortality is of a type which should be within the reach of human beings too.

The hunger that weighs down these generations is an expression not only of the actual state of physical want but also of their hunger for that which is lacking in quality. In these lines and in those that follow Keats displays a profound sense of history. Human history has been deviating from nature for a long time. The hungry generations are both the prisoners of want and the preservers of beauty, the nightingale's song. Thus the verse which sets out to celebrate the bird's immortality demonstrates equally **human** immortality. The appreciation of beauty has helped humanity survive throughout the hungry generations. (Cf. **Endymion**, I, 1 - 33 on the necessity of beauty for human survival.) Thus, the nightingale's voice ties the lyrical subject to the whole of the past:

> *The voice I hear this passing night was heard*
> *In ancient days by emperor and clown:*
> *Perhaps the self-same song that found a path*
> *Through the sad heart of Ruth, when, sick for home,*
> *She stood in tears amid the alien corn;*
> *The same that oft-times hath*
> *Charm'd magic casements, opening on the foam*
> *Of perilous seas, in faery lands forlorn.*

The first image indicates social **breadth** and **manifoldness**: the nightingale's song touches a chord in every human heart. *"Emperor and clown"* encompasses a whole series of polarities but also a certain community.

The succeeding more extensive and imaginatively more specific image of Ruth indicates the **depth** of the song's effect. The view zooms in from the general social level to the intensely personal, picking a familiar figure for the reader to relate to. (Keats' imaginative recreation of Ruth, however, does not correspond to the Bible.) The nightingale's song found a path into Ruth's heart as it was to do so much later into the lyrical subject's. Sensuous beauty is perceived through the human heart (i.e. emotionally) and flooding out from there affects the whole of the personality. This is also its effect on the lyrical subject, whom the *"self-same song"* reminds of common humanity. The emotional community between Ruth, the lyrical subject, Keats and the reader is achieved through powerful evocation. *"Sad heart"* adds a highly personal dimension to the familiar biblical story. The metrical retardation in this phrase[47] underlines the elegiac mood of the whole image. With a simple change of word order in *"sick for home"* - so much more potent than 'homesick' - Keats paves the way emotionally for the final line of the image, stressing Ruth's utter loneliness with which the lyrical subject can so easily empathize.

The third and final image of this stanza differs qualitatively from the previous two. While those heighten the awareness of common humanity, the concluding image indicates that there is also a response to the song which can lead away from humanity into barren places. Despite this they exercise a magical allure - one reason why they are so *"perilous"*. This is the other possible function of the nightingale's song, dangerous, tempting, 'treasonable'.

Both functions are possible and both occur within this ode as well as within the English Romantic movement. The lyrical subject too was attracted initially by the nightingale's 'promise' of fairy lands. He was almost ready to jump into the foam. Only now, with *"forlorn"*, the spell is broken and the lyrical subject becomes fully conscious of the implications of his attempted flight. This is the final step in returning to cold actuality. Flight with the nightingale - as he now understands - causes separation from humanity and thus in a complex way finally means the loss of sensuous perception of life's beauty. Beauty, despite the constant threat of its decay, is inextricably rooted in life. Along with the desire to leave the world the nightingale's song has stimulated the lyrical subject's imagination into creating visions of life's potential, utopias, which overcome the deficiencies of historical reality. In the last analysis these utopian visions serve to bind the lyrical subject, poet and reader closer to life and contribute towards the realisation that beauty and material life are inseparable.

Critical opinion on this stanza is most diverse when it comes to the image of the casements. Few are prepared to recognise the qualitative difference between it and the preceding two images which has been seen to be of considerable importance. Thus R. H. Fogle writes about the magic casements as

> (...) *the apex and climax of the imaginative experience. They are deliberately towering and frail, dramatizing the value, the galantry, and the precariousness of the Romantic imagination at its height. They are connected with the actual by defying it, by their affirmation that what the mind can imagine is beauty and truth (...)* [48]

There is certainly a strong connection between these windows and the possibilities of the imagination. This enchanting vision is created by the imagination. But if this image is part and parcel of the ode's message then it must contribute in one way or another to the argument. Stanza VII, and in particular this final image, induce the lyrical subject to abandon his desire to leave the world. This cannot be brought about merely by an abstract imaginative quality. It is because these casements are so alluring that they have so much power in tempting one to turn one's back on human concerns and thus on life's dynamic beauty.

Those critics who, like Wasserman, work from the preconceived notion that two mutually exclusive worlds exist side by side, the non-human nightingale's world being the unquestionably superior one, naturally view the *"faery lands"* in the same light, despite textual difficulty in accommodating such a reading:

> *The fairy lands are "forlorn" because they must be lost to man so long as he is in the mortal world. They are the mystery, but they cannot be peopled by mortals, for human existence involves an ignorance of the mystery even though the mystery is the central principle of man's life.* [49]

Donal Wesling attempts a Marxist analysis in the sense of concentrating on the historical aspect of the imagery:

In an earlier time in European history, the artist-minstrel had a combined audience of emperor and serf, but now such a national audience is broken into fragments. Keats proceeds even further, then, back as far as Biblical history. But he lights upon Ruth, favoring not a figure of the social establishment (Isaac, or Jacob) but someone unconventional, a displaced person, a Biblical type of wanderer. (...) He presses further in this amazing regressive stanza, piling up rich epithets, overloading syntax and diction alike in the "magic casements" lines, so to convey the poetic transport of the "faery lands" of prehistory. The regression in time and space is complete. Yet "forlorn": forlorn are those faery lands because uninhabited by real humans, and in them there can be no forging of consciousness or conscience, no self-creation. In VIII, then, the return is inevitable to self-critique and the deflation of "fancy". [50]

The idea is interesting in itself and coincides with my interpretation at certain points, but as Wesling misses the crucial difference between the first two images and the third he is forced into the construction of a rather tenuous thesis of the fairy land's location in prehistory. There is no textual foundation for such an assumption.

VIII

The exclamatory repetition of *"forlorn"* - the full meaning of which is grasped by the lyrical subject only when the word is pronounced - intensifies emotionally the poem's final turning-point.

Forlorn! the very word is like a bell
To toll me back from thee to my sole self!

The very sound of the words indicates this tolling back to life. The

ODE TO A NIGHTINGALE

repetition of *"Adieu"* in line 5 indicates a clean break with the nightingale. The lyrical subject contemplates its departure philosophically:

> *Adieu! the fancy cannot cheat so well*
> *As she is fam'd to do, deceiving elf.*
> *Adieu! adieu! thy plaintive anthem fades*
> *Past the near meadows, over the still stream,*
> *Up the hill-side; and now 'tis buried deep*
> *In the next valley-glades:*
> *Was it a vision, or a waking dream?*
> *Fled is that music: - Do I wake or sleep?*

The statement concerning fancy's inability to deceive as well as *"she is fam'd to do"* is lightly ironical, reinforcing the emotional self-distancing. It is also further proof that the second attempt at flight, through the poetic imagination, is indeed a far more extensive and serious endeavour than merely one of two lines. Only now, after the full realisation of the consequences of such an escape can the lyrical subject dismiss fancy.

The following images trace the growing spatial self-removal of the bird. Not the nightingale but its song is watched disappearing. While the meadows are *"near"*, *"still stream"* implies greater distance, as the eye can no longer perceive the water's movement. The next landmark needs to be larger to be seen (*"hill-side"*) and further flight can only be imagined. *"Buried deep"* indicates that the song has died away. With the departure of the song the point of reference around which the ode's struggle has revolved also disappears. It is no longer necessary and the lyrical subject is no longer attracted to it. He finds himself in a new day. On this level too the poem's development can be traced. In stanzas IV (*"Queen-Moon"*) and VI it is night. The importance of stanza VI in the inner struggle is, as I pointed out earlier, underlined by the reference to midnight. Stanza VII, in which the decision taken in stanza VI is further strengthened, is associated with night beginning to come to an end in *"this passing night"*. The visual description of the song's disappearance, finally, is only possible after day-break. (Awakening as an image of return to cold reality out of an enchanted dream is also to be found in **La**

Belle Dame Sans Merci, XI, 3-4: *"And I awoke and found me here / On the cold hill-side."* - it too was written in April / May 1819).

The nightingale and the song are fled, so is the great attraction they held for the lyrical subject. The music of the ode itself comes to an end with this departure. The finality of this is accentuated by the emphasis given to *"Fled"*. What degree of reality can be attributed to the experience? The questions at the end of **Ode to a Nightingale** are reminiscent of those concluding **A Midsummer Night's Dream**.[51]

A resolution of these questions does not materially influence the 'message' of the ode as a whole. Here they express the lyrical subject's uncertainty and the necessity to find new bearings in reality. Wesling comments: it is *"an open-endedness which is by implication anti-Classical."* [52]

The most common critical premise concerning this final stanza is the lyrical subject's 'loss' at having to return to reality from a 'better world'. Wasserman writes:

> *(...) if we assume that true "life" is experiencing the condition of heaven's bourne, then the nightingale "lives" on earth but the poet cannot; and the poet's return to this world is therefore a "dying" that is announced by the same death-knell that summons him back to what most men call "life".*[53]

In fact the ode has shown that the poet does not resign himself to a condition of death-in-life. The tension between the actual world and the world as it might be indicates the necessity and possibility of changing the human condition through becoming aware of its potential. The possibility of change lies within life itself. This emerges in stanza III, where life alone brings forth Beauty and Love, even though they cannot survive for long. The poet as a lover of the sensous enjoyment of beauty must hate the world that brings forth beauty only to destroy it. But as beauty and its appreciation are rooted in the actual world, he cannot flee from it. It is the beauty of the world which penetrates and 'takes over' the visions of stanzas II and V, thus confounding and subverting all attempts at escape. The visions of the 'other' world, brought about by the desire to escape, are in fact packed with the real, material world.

ODE ON A GRECIAN URN

Such dim-conceived glories of the brain
Bring round the heart an undescribable feud;
So do these wonders a most dizzy pain,
That mingles Grecian grandeur with the rude
Wasting of old Time - with a billowy main -
A sun - a shadow of a magnitude.

Despite the multitude of differing interpretations it appears to be widely accepted that **Ode on a Grecian Urn** demonstrates art's superiority over life.[54] What defines this superiority is a subject of debate. A crucial factor in the formation of critical opinion is whether the critic in question sees the ode as a poem of development, involving struggle and contradiction, or not. If the critic works from the hypothesis that no such struggle takes place then the statement in stanza I is taken as Keats' immutable opinion to be elaborated and embellished in what follows. On the other hand there are discerning critics who find reason to question the unqualified supremacy of the urn and there are even some who suggest that the poem's message points to quite the opposite, the supremacy of life.[55]

I hope to trace in my discussion the ode's development from visual art's unquestioned supremacy to an insight into the complexity of relations between art and life.

I

Thou still unravish'd bride of quietness,
Thou foster-child of silence and slow time,

The opening address celebrates essential qualitites of the urn as a work of visual art. In contrast to music, for instance, it is closely related to quietness and silence, through the words *"bride"* and *"foster-child"*, and its own muteness is suggested in the ambiguity of *"still"* as well as the poet's inner monologue, which is part of the general quiet.

Like all great works of art the urn is fostered and matured by *"slow time"*, proving its magnitude with the passing ages. The slowness of time passing is made perceptible in the sequence of two stressed syllables, *"slów-tíme"*.[56]

Tension is created in the description of the urn as an *"unravish'd bride"* - a deliberately impermanent condition - conflicting with the eternity of the urn, i.e. the eternity of this impermanent condition. The tension is heightened by *"still"* in its uppermost meaning of 'yet'. This suggests the possibility that the urn may be ravished, even though its permanence negates this possibility. In the terms of art *"unravish'd"* indicates that the urn's secret has not been revealed. In this lies the guarantee for its lastingness as a work of art, its continued challenge to those who contemplate it. In this light the seemingly paradoxical combination of *"unravish'd bride"* and eternity makes sense. It lies within the nature of great art that it can never be fully explained for all time, its complex associations finally 'rationalised' in their entirety. It has something new to say to every generation in addition to what it told their predecessors. Thus the urn presents a challenge to each new generation and the fact that the poet sees it as an *"unravish'd bride"* indicates his own desire to discover its secret.

The transition from calmly addressing the urn to wishing to penetrate its secret gains impetus with the change of rhythm within the first quatrain. The first two lines are endstopped and begin on an unstressed syllable. They are marked by a regular rhythm which underlines the poet's calm certainty. This regularity is broken up by the subsequent shift of stress to the first syllable of line 3 and by the faster flow of speech made necessary by the two unstressed syllables between the stresses:

Sýlvàn hìstórìàn, who canst thus express
A flowery tale more sweetly than our rhyme:

While the lyrical subject[57] at first addresses the urn as a passive object, the view now focuses on its active capacity as a work of visual art, distinct from poetry (*"our rhyme"*). Grammatically this change is reflected in the occurrence of the first verb, *"express"*. At the same time the idea of the urn's silence is subtly modified; *"historian"* and *"tale"* undermine the impression of a total lack of sound: the urn's silence is only at the acoustic level. To the lyrical subject this seems an advantage over verse, his own form of art.

"Sylvan" is the first allusion to the urn's frieze and creates the vision of open woodland and pagan deities. *"Flowery tale"* and *"leaf-fring'd legend"* deepen these associations, suggesting at the same time a highly decorated tale.

> *What leaf-fring'd legend haunts about thy shape*
> *Of deities or mortals, or of both,*
> *In Tempe or the dales of Arcady?*

"Haunts", like *"express"*, applies to the frieze, stressing its mobility and indicating the lyrical subject's initial difficulty in clearly grasping the depicted scenes. The question, as it develops over three lines, gives an increasingly clear idea of the subject matter of the frieze. The initial uncertainty concerning the depicted figures' human or extra-human nature is maintained in the concluding line of the question: both Tempe and Arcady, places of beauty traditionally associated with pastoral poetry, harbour deities and mortals alike.

In the remaining three lines of the stanza more questions conjure up a vivid picture:

> *What men or gods are these? What maidens loth ?*
> *What mad pursuit ? What struggle to escape ?*
> *What pipes and timbrels ? What wild ecstasy ?*

The first of these six questions does not differ in content from that part of the previous one concerning the protagonists. Nonetheless there has been a significant change. First, the more abstract terms of Latin origin, *"deities or mortals"*, have been replaced by more familiar words derived from Anglo-Saxon, *"men or gods"*. This makes it easier to relate to the figures. Secondly, the reversal of their order suggests the likelihood that the figures are human. This feeling becomes a growing certainty with the following question *"What maidens loth?"*. And *"loth"* prepares the way for the coming scene of pursuit and escape. The concentration of two densely phrased questions per line contributes to the growing impression of speed, as does the pipe and timbrel music, typical of the Bacchus cult. The image created is one of acceleration, sensual pleasure and music, culminating in *"wíld écstàsy"*, which retards the tempo at the point of climax, rather than hastening it.

Seven questions have made the frieze come alive. It contains images of abundance, fertility and joy-in-life, values immensely attractive to Keats, who saw them as the way life should be. The vivid movement depicted on the frieze, its capturing of a fleeting moment, are merged with the silence, immobility and eternity of the urn. This fusion creates a tension which can be compared to the condition of the eternally unravished bride, a feeling of halted movement. Yet this differs from the arrestation of movement which we noted in the opening stanza of **Ode to Pysche**. There the life of nature **went on**, if at a more cautious pace, and the images captured this movement. Here, in **Ode on a Grecian Urn**, all movement has been fixed, in accordance with the form of art, which cannot preserve process.[58] The feeling of halted movement is conveyed on the stylistic level by the use of nouns instead of verbs to express action. Thus the reader is left with a complex impression of arrested action, of generated, 'frozen' energy.

There is a marked tendency among literary critics to attribute supernatural powers to the urn. One of the best known exponents of this approach is Wasserman who uses the ode to illustrate his own mystic philosophy. His initial conception of the urn as something supernatural leads him to extreme conclusions:

> *But the urn only approaches this region*[59], *since the statement that it is **still** unravished carries with it the threat that it eventually may be ravished, and since it is related to slow*

time rather than to no-time. The deceleration is only moving the urn in the direction of the extra-temporal.[60]

Mayhead - who reads the text in general far more closely than his US colleague - also starts his analysis from the hypothesis that the urn possesses superhuman qualities:

If the urn is more pure than humanity, it is also a better and sweeter story-teller than the human poet.[61]

There is no indication in the text that the urn has divine qualities. The opening lines relate strictly to qualities of the urn as a work of visual art, followed by a comparison to the art of verse. At this stage in the poem the lyrical subject sees the visual form of art as superior to his own. This is the starting point of a struggle that will develop throughout the poem and must not be taken to be Keats' final opinion. If the initial statement is divorced from the poem's struggle then the subsequent conflict loses all significance and the ode's 'message' will become virtually impossible to grasp.

I have indicated in the previous chapters that Keats' visions of the way life should be often are marked by fertility, plenty and energy. The scenes depicted on the urn's frieze contain precisely these things. However, in contrast to stanza V of the **Nightingale**, Keats, in the images of the urn, indicates abscence of process. What the lyrical subject does not yet fully realise, Keats captures by showing the scenes to be movement arrested, simultaneously dynamic and immobile. The main conflict of the ode is already indicated.

II

Movement, music, esctasy are followed by quiet, sober contemplation. The lyrical subject has become sufficiently familiar with the frieze to take a look at individual scenes. The short, successive questions touched on different facets catching the eye and thus created an impression of the urn revolving. Now it seems to have come to a standstill.

ODE ON A GRECIAN URN

> *Heard melodies are sweet, but those unheard*
> *Are sweeter; therefore, ye soft pipes, play on;*
> *Not to the sensual ear, but, more endear'd,*
> *Pipe to the spirit ditties of no tone:*

Both *"Heard"* and *"unheard"* carry particular stress, created by accent and their positioning at each end of the line. Once more the superiority of visual art over another form of art - this time music - is celebrated. The difference between the two, it is said, lies in the fact that one becomes material reality, the other is realised imaginatively. The latter is preferred. This **observation** on the specific quality of both these forms of art is perfectly valid, whereas the **evaluation** is a deliberate part of the exposition. Interpretations that incline towards a 'spiritualisation' of the urn ignore this parallel between the first quatrains of stanzas I and II - the comparsions between the urn and other forms of art, verse (stanza I) and music (stanza II). Thus remarks such as Bate's *"the urn's silence in ordinary human terms"* [62] depart from what the text actually says. The difference made here is clearly that between acoustically and imaginatively realised music, the latter appearing superior at this point. The music of the preceding stanza - *"What pipes and timbrels"*, real as it seemed, came alive only through Keats' imagination. This concurrence of the audible and inaudible, which was simply a natural part of the poetic experience in stanza I, is now reflected upon. The contradiction is expressed in *"soft pipes, play on"*, *"Pipe"* and *"ditties"*, the words themselves suggesting the sound which is then negated by *"of no tone"*. Such reflections on the possibilities of visual art is nothing new or strange to Keats.[63]

The introductory reflection is followed by the depiction of a scene containing a singing youth. While the theme of music is continued, the focus changes from music as such to the person creating it.

> *Fair youth, beneath the trees, thou canst not leave*
> *Thy song, nor ever can those trees be bare;*

More important, however, is the change in the lyrical subject's sentiment. Although the concurrence of the audible and inaudible is continued, the supremacy of the inaudible and therefore unceasing music is questioned. The ceaselessness of the song is also conveyed by the enjambment. Even though the youth is depicted at a highpoint of creativity *"canst not"* brings home the static or fixed nature of his condition, taking away some of its attraction.

This idea is repeated in the closely connected image of the trees. They too have been fixed at a kind of climax - that of abundance and fertility - and thus are deprived of the natural process on which their fertility is based. This idea was to be more fully explored and developed by Keats in **To Autumn**. There is a slight shift in emphasis inside the images of the singer and the trees: while the singer cannot leave the summit of his achievement, the trees can never experience the barrenness of winter. The price for maintaining this peak is the surrender of the fleetingness that makes or defines a true culmination. Because the natural process has been halted it can never turn into its opposite. Both conditions, the climax - unceasing song - and the anti-climax - bareness of trees -, have been ambiguously evaluated through the negative expressions *"canst not"* and *"nor ever can"*. The climax becomes almost undesirable while the anti-climax seems desirable. Thus the previous declaration about visual art's supremacy over other art forms is put into question. Music, it is suggested, might after all be a truer sensuous culmination than the visual image of a musician, and verse could perhaps better encompass life's process. The image of the trees introduces the implicit contrast and confrontation of visual art and life. This transition to the main theme of the ode - a weighing up of the different values of life and the arts - is completed in the extensive final image of this stanza:

> *Bold Lover, never, never canst thou kiss,*
> *Though winning near the goal - yet, do not grieve;*
> *She cannot fade, though thou hast not thy bliss,*
> *For ever wilt thou love, and she be fair!*

ODE ON A GRECIAN URN

Again there is a shift of emphasis, while preserving the theme of the ambiguity of life's fixation through visual art. Now it is not the culmination that is fixed but the moment preceding it. Thus the shifting balance between positive and negative in the 'freezing' of life through art seems almost on the verge of toppling, with a contrary view to that of lines I, 1 - II, 4 making itself felt. Emotionally, too, this overbalancing is being prepared. The impression of anxiety over art's arresting of life's process is intensified by the repetition of *"never"*. The image is so vivid in its precision that the lyrical subject comes close to rejecting the fixation of life through art.

The caesura which follows shows that the lyrical subject has emotionally distanced himself from the lover and is trying to rationalise the positive side of art. Even so *"yet do not grieve"* suggests that there may be grounds for grief. The comfort offered in the concluding two lines is unconvincing: *"She cannot fade"* is but little consolation for the lover's great loss, even though *"cannot"* carries an unquestioned, positive meaning only here in contrast to its previous uses. Even the apparently unambiguous final line does not convince because this love will remain eternally unfulfilled.

In their discussions of this stanza the critics are largely concerned about the introductory statement and the relationship between the scenes on the urn and real life.

Wasserman, in his interpretation of stanza I, had taken the urn to represent the immortal and the frieze temporality.[64] In stanza II, Wasserman writes,

> *(...) the immortal-essential and the temporal-physical (converge) towards a point of fusion where these categorical distinctions are blotted out.* [65]

At the opening of stanza II

> *The silence of the urn and the sound of the pipes and timbrels have run together* [66]

according to Wasserman. In fact the only thing that changes between stanza I and the opening of stanza II is that the dramatic monologue moves from a vivid portrayal of the urn to a contemplation of its abilities. The pipes and timbrels are already tied to the urn's silence in stanza I. It is Keats' creative power that makes the reader 'forget' this inaudibility.

Neither can one agree with Wasserman's identification of the urn with the immortal, the frieze with the temporal. The frieze carries the message of this work of art and it is here that action has been 'frozen'. It is not a question of the frieze and the urn converging but of real life and the powers of art doing so to form an image of life arrested. The images of the second half of stanza II have at least put a question mark against the desirability of this convergence.

The struggle of opposites which the critic recognises as existing in the first stanza is not confined to it but develops throughout the ode. How this contradiction manifests itself within the second stanza I have tried to point out. It is this conflict that pushes on the poem's action. The contradictory images, the uneasiness expressed at that which has just been unequivocally hailed, are crucial to an understanding of the ode.

Patterson, who breaks with the traditional view of the ode celebrating art's superiority over life, tends to overemphasise the opposite, i.e. that Keats shows from the very beginning of the poem the supremacy of life.[67] The critic thus impedes his own perception of the conflict. If the lyrical subject were convinced of life's superiority from the very outset, the struggle he goes through would be a mere pretence and of no real significance to the reader. Patterson takes this position in the course of his polemic with the traditional view.[68] One can, however, go along with the critic when he says:

At the risk of being labelled a Freudian, I earnestly contend that there is as much eulogy of passion as of permanence in the Ode. Failure to recognize both in their proper relationship results in this type of "broken-back" reading - an interpretation which cannot embrace the whole and which must therefore condemn a part of the poem to save itself. Such a reading reduces the poem to a simple lyric of escape and makes of the poet a young man unwilling to face life as it is.[69]

III

Deliberately and pointedly turning away from the contradictions of stanza II the third opens on a note of almost blind enthusiasm:

Ah, happy, happy boughs! that cannot shed
Your leaves, nor ever bid the Spring adieu;
And, happy melodist, unwearied,
For ever piping songs for ever new;

What was previously viewed as rather a dubious advantage is now lauded without reservation. Again the musician and the lovers appear, in possession of that which the lyrical subject so fervently desires: eternal creativity and vitality. The forced suppression of the dialectics of stanza II makes itself felt in a marked decline in poetic quality. It is here, on this level, that one feels how much Keats is working out a problem that affected him personally in writing the ode.

"*Happy*" is used excessively in an attempt to express what cannot be convincingly conveyed in the language of imagery. All images here praise exclusively the 'positive' of the two sides contained in the previous stanza. The endless flow of creative activity is stressed only in its attraction. Repetition of *"for ever"* conveys a growing emotional involvement. This affirmation of the eternity of a desired, and in real life all too fleeting state culminates in the passionate outburst

More happy love! more happy, happy love!

This threefold repetition of *"happy"* in one line not only expresses the lyrical subject's aroused emotions, as he clings to the idea of art's supremacy, but also indicates the exhaustion of Keats' artistic means. In order to show convincingly the superiority of 'art-love' he is forced to depart from the scene and supplement art with qualities taken from 'life-love':

> *For ever warm and still to be enjoy'd,*
> *For ever panting, and for ever young;*

Suddenly 'art-love' receives a vibrant, sensual reality which captures the reader's imagination. Both *"warm"* and *"panting"*, the most powerfully attractive qualities, are however alien to the marble coldness of the urn. These are sensations to be experienced in life alone. Only this fusion of life and art can bring about a convincing superiority of art! What was previously regarded a severe disadvantage (*"never canst thou kiss"*) is now put forward as a situation of expectancy: *"still to be enjoy'd"*. But this implies the impossible - this scene of love can never be brought to a culmination but only be forever anticipated. The single quality which is in complete compliance with the possibilities of visual art is *"for ever young"*.

This interlocking of art and life which Keats has to undertake in order to achieve a viable superiority of art is never commented on in traditional criticism.

The image of 'art-love' - subtly enriched with qualities taken from life - is now contrasted with that aspect of the human experience of love which is uppermost on the lyrical subject's mind:

> *All breathing human passion far above,*
> *That leaves a heart high-sorrowful and cloy'd,*
> *A burning forehead, and a parching tongue.*

"Breathing" signifies the contrast to lifeless art. It also emphasises the point that *"panting"* can only be a human sensation. *"Panting"* captures the reader's imagination more than *"breathing"* because of its intensely passionate associations. Breathing human love is shown in its effect on the 'seat of passion', on the heart, and then on the physical condition of human lovers. Both *"high-sorrowful"* and *"cloy'd"* are vivid and charged with unpleasant emotions unknown to the lovers on the urn. The emotional component is upheld and amplified in the

images of the final line. While *"breathing"* does not reach the intensity of its counterpart *"panting"* , *"burning"* and *"parching"* appeal more acutely to the senses and are more vivid than *"warm"*. The unity of emotion and sensuousness in the images reaches its peak here, at the end of stanza III, a culmination brought about by the experience of life itself. In this way the stanza which started off unconvincingly recovers in its second half to reach a new, sensuously more complex quality of vividness, different from that of stanzas I and II.

In this stanza Keats' thinking in images is developed to an extraordinary degree. It is important to realise that the images in fact undermine the lyrical subject's verbal affirmation of visual art's superiority. This is the realisation that the stanza brings about, defining its place in the ode's developing logic. The insistence on superiority fails and so the lyrical subject has to turn to a new scene on the frieze to grapple once more with the urn's silence and eternity.

The critics are often somewhat at a loss with the third stanza and its specific function within the ode as a whole. Frequently it is interpreted as a continuation or repetition of the previous stanza because the contradictions in the latter were not sufficiently recognised. Thus William Walsh writes in his chapter on Keats in **The Pelican Guide to English Literature** after having discussed the opening quatrain of the second stanza:

> *At this point, music comes to stand for the perfection of the possible, for all that is superior to 'the sensual ear'. The second half of this stanza and the whole of the third stanza detail the conclusion and connect it with the instances cut in the vase - the fair youth, the trees, the bough, the happy melodist.*[70]

While recognising the artistic decline in stanza III, the critic excludes the possibility of this performing a certain role within the developing logic of the poem. He sees in it a *"dimming of his critical conscience which leaves him unaware of the touch of caricature, of absurdity"*[71] rather than a weakness arising necessarily from one-sideness.

Wasserman sees no weakening in the artistic quality of the ode whatever. On the contrary, he reads the third stanza as the height of poetic experience! The lyrical subject (for Wasserman identical with Keats!) has supposedly reached *"heaven's bourne"*:

> *Finally, in the third stanza he has fully entered into the dynamically static existence of the symbols themselves as he does not merely address them, but, by means of the ecstatic exclamations, participates in their sensations and experiences.*[72]

And further down:

> *The poet, ecstatically unselfed into the symbols, is now partaking of the essence of life.*[73]

In this way the critic arrives at the conclusion that it is already here that *"beauty is truth"*.[74] Anticipating the question as to why this insight is not pronounced now, thus winding up the poem at the end of stanza III, Wasserman writes: *"he has stumbled"* and returns from 'heaven's bourne' to earth.[75] Such a reading is made possible by completely disregarding the text and the nature of the imagery. In fact through grappling with art's beauty the lyrical subject has come to realise the opposite: that the beauty he seeks cannot be found in art alone nor does it exist divorced from life. While to Wasserman 'heaven's bourne' is

> *that fine edge between mortal and immortal where passion is so intense that it refines itself into the essence of ecstasy, which is without passion*[76]

the lyrical subject is initially attracted to the vase by the eternity of the passions it depicts. The uneasy feeling which develops in the course of the second stanza and implicitly in the imagery of stanza III is based on the insight that art's sensuousness ultimately lacks life's warm vitality.

IV

At the end of stanza III the lyrical subject is left in a state of indecision and must turn to a new scene on the urn if he wants to resolve the conflict.

The fourth stanza asks questions - the first since stanza I - once again serving to outline the scene:

Who are these coming to the sacrifice?
To what green altar, O mysterious priest,
Lead'st thou that heifer lowing at the skies,
And all her silken flanks with garlands drest?

The former ambivalence concerning the depiction of gods or men is now replaced by clearly human activities. The opening line is most evocative, *"coming to"* implying the lyrical subject's direct participation in the scene, as though he was already at the place of sacrifice and the people were approaching him. The following question is a combination of what is seen on the urn - the sharply etched image of the heifer - and a place not depicted on it - the altar - that arises in Keats' imagination. In contrast to the first question, *"Who are these"*, the second question is specifically addressed to the priest, who thus becomes part of the reader's imaginative picture of the scene on the urn. It also deepens the lyrical subject's own involvement in this scene.

"Green altar", both vivid and vague, underlines the paganism of the anticipated open air ritual. The description of the heifer which follows is the most extensive of the stanza. Its precise and intensely evocative depiction makes it the emotional centre of the entire verse, focusing all the reader's sympathy on it. *"Lowing"* introduces a completely new kind of sound into the frieze. The fear and helplessness of this cry are emotionally deepened by their contrast with the vastness of the skies, whose endlessness is underlined by the use of the plural. There is, as it were, a stark contradiction between the terrified heifer and its own outward appearance which is greatly enhanced in its vividness by the tactile component contained in *"silken"*. This tactile sense gives the reader the actual 'feel' of the animal and brings it closer still.

The third and last question of stanza IV, along with its accompanying statement, refers to something quite separate from the scene on the frieze:

What little town by river or sea shore,
Or mountain-built with peaceful citadel,
Is emptied of this folk, this pious morn?
And, little town, thy streets for evermore
Will silent be; and not a soul to tell
Why thou art desolate, can e'er return.

The various possible locations of the town make it impossible to assume that it is actually on the frieze. The depicted scene stimulates the poet's imagination into creating new scenes on the basis of the work of art. This demonstrates a great achievement of art. The urn and the scenes depicted on its frieze have come alive through Keats' imagination and now induce his fancy to further flights, to imagine beyond the imagined.

The anticipation of an empty town remains at the centre of interest to the end of the stanza. Like the preceding question, *"To what green altar..."*, this new question starts with an evocative description of what is in fact unknown, not being depicted on the urn. Thus the reader's imagination too is further stimulated by a combination of precision and vagueness in the description. Its elements - *"little"*, *"by river or sea shore"*, *"Or mountain-built with peaceful citadel"* - evoke distinct images, while the different possibilities create an overall impression which is relatively vague. This feeling of precision in the parts is perhaps one reason why a number of critics presume that the town can in fact be seen on the urn.[77]

The final statement abandons the immediacy and dynamism of the questions in favour of contemplative distance. The questions stressed movement as such rather than its fixation in the scenes. This was conveyed for instance by the use of verbs in the present tense instead of nouns. The present form also suggests that the action is eternally in progress, 'frozen' on to the urn. Due to the use of verbs, however, this static element is not as prominent as it was in stanza I, for instance, as this might impede the reader's sensuous perception of and emotional involvement in the scene. Moreover a simple return to the second stanza would have meant an artistically unfeasible repetition of the position before the beginning of stanza III. Thus the mobility of the scenes of stanza IV is in the last three lines proved to be just as fixed as earlier. In this way what is negative has also been fixed for ever. The heifer's fearful lowing will continue without end as does the piping, the town will for ever be emptied of its inhabitants, just as the lovers eternally 'love'. The conviction expressed at the outset of the ode - that visual art can *"thus express / A flowery tale more sweetly than our rhyme"* - is put into question. Here the poet feels the urn's inability to tell a tale (*"not a soul to tell / Why thou art desolate..."*). *"For evermore / Will silent be"* brings home the implication of life's fixation through visual art. This idea of loss through fixation is maintained to the end. The final lines thus create a complex, contradictory impression of the eternity and silence of the urn, strongly suggesting a critical distancing from the positions of stanzas I and III.

"Desolate" has a similar effect to *"forlorn"* in the **Nightingale,** implying solitariness, barrenness, disconsolateness. At the end of stanza IV - at the end also of the ode's actual struggle - it cannot be said that the poet has arrived at a simple solution. The initial appeal of visual art is now shown to determine its incompleteness, its 'perfection' determines its imperfection. The real experience of dynamism and fulfilment cannot be separated from life's process. It is a great achievement of art - both of visual art (the urn) and of verse (the ode) - to induce such an awareness. Art's beauty has made the lyrical subject aware of life's beauty and made him understand that an escape into the beauty of art would mean a severe loss. But neither the beauty of art nor that of life can be neglected. Each sharpens the senses for the beauty of the other.

The majority of those critics whose interpretations are based on the received opinion that the ode celebrates the superiority of art over life and who have therefore blinded themselves to the contradictions expressed in the struggle between art and life in stanzas I - III findsthemselves left with little option but to continue to ignore this struggle, a struggle which reaches its culmination in the fourth stanza. Bate writes:

> *The second and especially the third stanzas have been a digression. We have only to apply the simple test of omitting them both, or else the third alone, and we find that what remains will still make a complete poem, though admittedly less rich. On the other hand, if we keep all the others and omit the fourth, or if we simply glance at the close of the third and the opening of the fifth, we can see that there would be no transition at all and that, in the third stanza, Keats has found himself moving away from the principle feelings that the urn at first suggested to him: a receptive delight in its permanence of form, its mystery and inscrutability. Hence the primary function of the fourth stanza is to return more concretely to the Grecian urn and to some of the feelings that were present at the start.* [78]

Thus Bate, like some other critics, treats the poem as an uncontrolled act of inspiration rather than a carefully wrought work of art: he sees no development inside the ode at all! The unfortunate deviation - in the eyes of the critic - may be omitted and is finally overcome by the poet's fortunate return to the congenial position expressed at the opening of the poem. The struggle and dialectics of the ode, those two qualities which define its greatness, are thus painlessly removed. **Ode on a Grecian Urn**, like **Ode to a Nightingale**, is among the greatest poems in the English language precisely because of this intense struggle fought out in it, because of the dialectical structure of its images which forbids a mechanical supremacy of either art or life. Critics who attempt to water down or even remove these qualities seriously impede a recognition of the magnitude of Keats' poetry.

V

The fifth stanza opens on a note of emotional detachment. The inner struggle comes to a close at the end of stanza IV with the complex position that neither art nor life are perfect, that they need one another. Any return to a mechanical assumption of the supremacy of art would mean a step backwards. The final verse must therefore serve to expand on this position. The understanding has so far been conveyed in the language of images. Stanza V sets out to elaborate this insight on a more abstract level of thought. The lyrical subject thus returns to a view of the urn as a whole. This provokes a comparison with stanza I which is also recalled by the identity of rhyme scheme in the sestets (abc bac), differing from those of stanza II (abc acb) and stanzas III and IV (abc abc). There is a strong contrast between stanzas I and V in the degree of emotional involvement. The final stanza addresses the urn in a tone of playful alliteration: *"O Attic shape! Fair attitude"*. The urn no longer has the same compelling attraction. The ease with which the poet can now treat it arises from having met the urn's challenge and grappled with it. Nevertheless its silence and dignity are preserved. *"Attitude"* contains the idea of stasis. Any possible lingering doubt as to the identity of the figures is removed:

> *with brede*
> *Of marble men and maidens overwrought,*
> *With forest branches and the trodden weed;*

Comparison with stanza I serves only to stress the familiarity with which the poet can now address the urn. The images emerge more concretely and are thus closer to life. Yet unlike the fourth stanza the fifth leaves no room for life's warmth: *"marble"* qualifies the vividness and shows that it is frozen, cold and hard. The tactile component involved in *"marble"* - clearly contrasting with *"silken"* - intensifies this impression, creating a complex rational-sensory quality. It would now be unthinkable to describe the figures as *"warm"* or *"panting"*, however, *"marble"* once more underlines the urn's beauty.

After a last look at the figures the eye turns to the vegetation which has gained in plasticity. *"Trodden weed"* seems to be semantically incompatible with *"marble"* but the grammatical form of the adjective creates a feeling of dynamic stasis. *"Overwrought"* suggests a highly decorated object as well as there being too much decoration for the poet to cope with.

Now the plasticity of the images retreats, making room for the longest reflection contained in the ode:

> *Thou, silent form, dost tease us out of thought*
> *As doth eternity: Cold Pastoral!*
> *When old age shall this generation waste,*
> *Thou shalt remain, in midst of other woe*
> *Than ours, a friend to man, to whom thou say'st,*
> *"Beauty is truth, truth beauty," - that is all*
> *Ye know on earth, and all ye need to know.*

The urn as a work of art is now seen in its specific ability to draw the observer under its spell by the endless wealth of associations and thought which it stimulates. This it has in common with any great work of art. It can never be finally exhausted or 'explained' for all time. This is the abiding secret that can never be revealed or *"ravish'd"*. This too is why the urn *"tease(s) us out of thought/ As doth eternity"*.

The exclamation *"Cold Pastoral!"* underlines the conclusion arrived at by the lyrical subject, stressing the urn's lack of life's warmth. But the dialectical insight is not lost. The final lines demonstrate the importance of great art in human history. Like the nightingale's song it stimulates belief in humanity and life. Art like the bird's song brings about a consciousness of the warmth and dynamism of life which cannot be surpassed and for which there is no substitute. It provides the individual with strength to face life as it is and recognise its potential. This was experienced by the lyrical subject in both odes, creating an increasingly clear understanding that neither art nor nature, when cut off from life's dynamic process and the intense experience of sensuousness, can contain true beauty. It is 'perfection' that makes their beauty imperfect. Both the nightingale and the urn, which at first tempt the lyrical subject to escape, serve to heighten his awareness of the beauty and dynamism of life thus binding him closer to the earth. This was only achieved by grappling with and overcoming the attractions of escape.

It has emerged in stanza IV that art is instrumental in heightening the awareness of life's real and irreplaceable dynamism - the ultimate source of beauty, that highest quality of beauty. This beauty is the essential truth of life. It is this beauty which is explored in the odes that follow. This beauty - which is life's truth - is the urn's message. The fact that the urn 'says' this message has caused much consternation. I do not see why it should. The urn has been expressing its 'tale' all along. As a result of trying to penetrate the urn's secret the lyrical subject reaches his conclusion. This is what the urn 'says' to him in its own wordless language.

The final comment *"that is all/ Ye know on earth, and all ye need to know"* has given rise to interpretations that imply a place superior to earth. But as I read it this statement is meant as a general truth about life, valid for everyone and at all times.

The immense variety of interpretations of these last lines forbids any attempt at discussing them in any detail here. The pendulum swings from T. S. Eliot's remarks that they are *"meaningless"* [79] to that trend in criticism which blinds itself to the ode's inner struggle in order to invent for itself that very supremacy of art which is so passionately debated and finally rejected in the poem. The latter see beauty as art's beauty, art's supremacy as truth. In the case of Wasserman, who identifies the urn with a superhuman mode of existence, this means that beauty and truth exist only outside and beyond human life, i.e. at 'heaven's bourne'.[80]

Such an interpretation is surely alien to Keats' immensely sensuous, life-affirming poetry.

The artificially imposed division into inferior life and superior art contains another danger: it could destroy the poet's anticipation of life's potential, which is the great message of the ode to the reader *"in midst of other woe"* who should take from it an understanding that any attempt to opt out of life is futile. In the final analysis criticism which conceals this message plays into the hands of those who wish to console us with a better life hereafter and thus stifle a constructive attitude to changing the world and making it more like the potential Keats envisioned.

ODE ON MELANCHOLY

Stop and consider! life is but a day;
A fragile dew-drop on its perilous way
From a tree's summit; a poor Indian's sleep
While his boat hastens to the monstrous steep
Of Montmorenci. Why so sad a moan?
Life is the rose's hope while yet unblown;
The reading of an ever-changing tale;
The light uplifting of a maiden's veil;
A pigeon tumbling in clear summer air;
A laughing school-boy, without grief or care,
Riding the springy branches of an elm.

(from **Sleep and Poetry**)

In contrast to **Ode to a Nightingale** and **Ode on a Grecian Urn**, the lyrical subject in **Ode on Melancholy** wages no inner struggle. The conflict has been resolved and, as the title indicates, melancholy is to be reflected upon, not exemplified.

Keats' grappling with melancholy at this stage is not entirely unmotivated. Reasons for it can be found in literary history and tradition, in the author's personal and philsophical development as well as in the outcome of the struggles in the two preceding odes.

A long tradition of two types of melancholy may be traced in English literature, 'sweet melancholy' and 'sad melancholy'. A combination of these is found in such famous examples as Burton's ***"Democritus to the reader"*** in the **Anatomy of Melancholy** and Milton's **Il Penseroso** and **L'Allegro**. Eighteenth century writers tended to stress the one side of this combination, 'sad melancholy', indulging in a contemplation of gloom and death, which found expression in the Graveyard school and even to a certain extent in the **Elegy Written in a Country Church-Yard**. Shelley, on the other hand, underlines in **A Defence of Poetry** the inseparability of *"pleasure in its* *highest sense*"[81] and melancholy. Keats' concept of melancholy is closely related to that of Shelley. It focuses on the intense experience of life's beauty.

From the odes already written there has emerged a concept of beauty inseparably linked to life. Keats now feels impelled to express this newly won conviction poetically.

Alongside **Ode on Melancholy** a stanza has been preserved which was probably originally intended to introduce the ode but then rejected:

> *Though you should build a bark of dead men's bones,*
> *And rear a phantom gibbet for a mast,*
> *Stitch creeds together for a sail, with groans*
> *To fill it out, blood-stained and aghast;*
> *Although your rudder be a dragon's tail*
> *Long sever'd, yet still hard with agony,*
> *Your cordage large uprootings from the skull*
> *Of bald Medusa, certes you would fail*
> *To find the Melancholy - whether she*
> *Dreameth in any isle of Lethe dull.*[82]

This stanza contains a large number of props usually associated with the Gothic novels and graveyard poetry, giving the verse an almost satirical tone. They are held together by the image of the boat, an image Keats frequently employs when writing about poetry.[83]

A comparison with the first stanza of the final version affords a striking contrast. While the rejected stanza somewhat mockingly alludes to two recent literary fashions the final version embraces a much broader and older tradition. It is built of images from Greek mythology and European flora and fauna traditionally found in melancholy verse. This is the literary legacy which Keats deems worthy of serious debate in an ode. The more earnest intent demands a more serious artistic treatment.

Stanza I opens with a vigorous rejection of a melancholy centered around death:

ODE ON MELANCHOLY

> *No, no, go not to Lethe, neither twist*
> *Wolf's-bane, tight-rooted, for its poisonous wine;*

The repetition of *"No"* and its echoes in the first half of line 1 serve to deepen the sense of urgency. *"Lethe"* is associated both with forgetfulness and death, a twofold reference which is renewed in *"poisonous wine"*. This sets the theme of stanza I.

"Twist" expresses exertion, and this is reinforced rhythmically: *"Wólf's-báne, tíght-roótèd, fòr its póisònòus wíne"*. This concentration of stressed syllables in the first half of the line conveys a feeling of density which substantiates *"twist"* and *"tight-rooted"*. The marked rhythmic change in the second half of the line anticipates the desired relief after the effort.

With *"wine"* an ambiguity enters into the image. While *"poisonous"* warns of the danger, the appeal of forgetfulness and death is conjured up in the description of the juice as wine. The combination and attraction of forgetfulness and death is reminiscent of **Ode to a Nightingale**. The poet is familiar with the type of melancholy alluded to from his own experience, and its appeal to him is made clear here.

The urgency and decisiveness of the opening lines carry an awareness of the danger of this temptation. Nonetheless, the deathly attraction remains throughout the first stanza. The contradictory appeal of this kind of melancholy is new compared to the rejected verse and creates a more complex attitude in the reader towards the poem's subject.

The initial adjuration not to induce death is continued in:

> *Nor suffer thy pale forehead to be kiss'd*
> *By nightshade, ruby grape of Proserpine;*

The new image, however, differs from its precursors in two ways. While the first two images were against the active inducement of melancholy, the third rejects its passive endurance. This death-centred melancholy is to be actively averted. Secondly, there is a shift from the physical to the mental: a crown made from the nightshade encircles the head. Although *"pale forehead"* underlines the sense of sickness and desolation it is not entirely negative; in fact *"kiss'd"* seems even more desirable than *"wine"*. The attraction of this kiss is heightened in *"ruby grape of Proserpine"*. *"Ruby"*, which is something of an opposite to *"pale"*, implies both beauty and preciousness. It seems to clash semantically with *"grape"*: while *"ruby"* suggests something hard, cold and certainly inedible, the opposite is true of *"grape"*. *"Ruby"* makes this grape inedible in spite of its attraction. Thus, *"ruby grape"* is ambivalent in a way comparable to the deadly appeal of *"poisonous wine"*. Temptation is increased in *"ruby grape"* because of the wider range of sensuous perceptions involved - touch is added to taste.

The second quatrain brings with it a change of a different kind. The classical allusions, which dominated the first four lines are now largely superseded by medieval emblems of melancholy:

> *Make not your rosary of yew-berries,*
> *Nor let the beetle, nor the death-moth be*
> *Your mournful Psyche, nor the downy owl*
> *A partner in your sorrow's mysteries;*

The worship of melancholy should not take the form of a death-wish, the poet objects, but this worship in itself is not rejected. Thus this quatrain contains the first clues to the poet's concept of true melancholy. As *"mournful Psyche"* - the only classical allusion in the quatrain - indicates, melancholy is a condition of the soul.

The suggestion of death and gloom are continued in the image of the owl, whose screech, supposedly announcing an impending death, secures its place in melancholy literature:

> *Bats, Owls the shady bowers over,*
> *In melancholy darkness hover.*[84]

Despite this connotation the owl is described invitingly as *"downy"*. It differs from the other images of this quatrain by possessing a sensuous quality - a softness inducing sleepiness. But this is a fairly mild attraction compared to the strong ambivalencies of the preceding quatrain.

The stanza's final two lines might be compared to the concluding couplet of a Shakespearean sonnet which usually comments on the preceding quatrains. Here they serve to underline the stanza's function as a proposition and express the poet's opinion on the problem raised:

For shade to shade will come too drowsily,
And drown the wakeful anguish of the soul.

The penultimate line makes clear the connection between the celebration of gloom and a slackening alertness of the senses. The repetition of *"shade"* and the alliteration of *"drowsily"* - *"drown"* introduce a monotony that seems to lull the senses into a state of sleepiness. The tendency to monotony stops with the clearest definition of true melancholy so far: *"the wakeful anguish of the soul"*. This formulation contrasts sharply with the false type of melancholy that induces the sleepiness of the senses. *"Wakeful"* and *"anguish"* counter the idea of forgetfulness, sleep and death, True melancholy requires complete mental and physical awareness and calls them into being in its turn. False melancholy would *"drown"* the perception for the true. The verb is strong in its irreversibility.

The necessity of conscious resistance to the lulling of mind and body is not only conveyed in the ideas, but also in the actual linguistic structures of the ode itself, as a practical example of the poet's opposition at this level. The vigorous opening and the number of run-on lines work against any feeling of tedium. Syntactical and rhythmical variety counteract the monotony which might have arisen from the constant negation of the various forms of misconceived melancholy.

In the stance taken here Keats has achieved a new stage in his own development since he wrote **Ode to a Nightingale** and **Ode on a Grecian Urn**.

Critics of this ode tend to dismiss the cancelled stanza as *"grim humour"* and *"clowning"*.[85] Although several of them comment on the antithetical structure of the poem as a whole,[86] few remark on the dissimilarity between the rejected stanza and stanza I in this respect.[87]

Garrod, Mayhead and Empson coincide in their views that the two types of melancholy differ in **quantity, not in quality**. Thus Garrod writes of *"that deeper and truer Melancholy which the Ode celebrates"* [88] and Mayhead comments:

> *(...) although the poem registers resistance, it is not resistance to melancholy itself but to the temptations which melancholy brings in its train (...)*[89]

Neither critic makes clear the essential difference between the one kind of melancholy which seeks forgetfulness and even death and the other kind which is set up as a direct contrast, culminating in *"the wakeful anguish of the soul"*. Garrod implies that the rejected melancholy is already deep and true, but the kind desired is even *"deeper and truer"* and Mayhead - though pointing out the necessity of resisting certain temptations - seems to be making the second quatrain, in which Keats warns against the piling up of emptied conventions, the exclusive basis for his interpretation.

Empson reads stanza I to the following effect:

> *Do not achieve death, or you can no longer live in its shadow. Taste rather at their most sharp the full sensations of death, of melancholy, and of oblivion. (...) there is no need for me to insist on the contrariety of the pathological splendours of this introduction.*[90]

Here the danger in understanding melancholy as something closely linked to thoughts of death is evident. This is exactly what Keats is rejecting. Empson, like Garrod, seems to suggest that there is no difference between the two types of melancholy regarding their orientation towards death. The coming stanza will have to confirm or disprove this. The first stanza with its rigorous repudiation of the cult of gloom, certainly puts a question mark against such an interpretation.

II

Stanza II forms a kind of antithesis to stanza I. Accordingly, its first quatrain considers the nature of true melancholy and how it arises:

But when the melancholy fit shall fall
Sudden from heaven like a weeping cloud,
That fosters the droop-headed flowers all,
And hides the green hill in an April shroud;

Melancholy is thus a natural phenomenon which descends suddenly and unsought for. It cannot be artificially created nor can it be avoided.

"But" announces the antithesis. *"Fit"* indicates that the melancholy mood takes hold of a person spontaneously and is not altogether desirable. Its likening to an April shower shows the mood's double nature: despite its description as a *"shroud"* the moist mist, clouding the hill's green protects it, nourishing the young grass.

After having said that melancholy should descend naturally and likening it to a phenomenon that **fosters life, not death,** the poet turns to a new aspect in the second part of the stanza:

Then glut thy sorrow on a morning rose,
Or on the rainbow of the salt sand-wave,
Or on the wealth of globed peonies;
Or if thy mistress some rich anger shows,
Emprison her soft hand, and let her rave,
And feed deep, deep upon her peerless eyes.

Again the antithetical parallel to stanza I is noticeable. Here the poet recommends responses adequate to the state of true melancholy. One should not try to avoid its effects but cultivate them to the full. The symbols of darkness and death are exchanged for images of light, brilliant colour and the living but transient beauty of nature.

The rose, traditional symbol of beauty, is caught at a moment of surpassing loveliness. The transcience of this moment - *"morning"* heightens its splendour, but also fosters melancholy.

The following image refers to an even more fleeting and unstable moment of supreme natural beauty: a rainbow in the surf. Keats' characteristic modification of a conventional phrase - here the 'salt sea wave' of the ballads - increases the density of the image. Apart from the brilliant visual 'freezing' of the water's movement (*"rainbow"*) *"salt sand"* appeals with a peculiar sharpness to the sense of taste. *"Salt sand-wave"* implies the wave's progress to its tide-mark on the beach, with accompanying suggestions of wetness, coolness and the tactile sensation of the damp sand. The simultaneous movement and its 'freezing' in this multisensory image makes it stand out with particular sharpness. At the same time this image differs from the others in that it enacts the movement from the culmination point of beauty to its turning to dust (*"sand-wave"*).

The colour spectrum of the rainbow epitomises the vastness of nature's possibilities. This inexhaustible wealth of nature, experienced acutely in such transient moments of intense natural beauty, is at the same time a guarantee that they will always recur. The experience and appreciation of the contradiction between beauty's intensity and its transcience is the generating point of melancholy. True melancholy is thus founded on the insight into the dialectics of life. And here lies its creative character, for it enables us to experience beauty with sharpened awareness.

The richness of nature's beauty is evoked even more directly, perhaps, in the stanza's third image: *"Or on the wealth of globed peonies"*. *"Globed"* 'fills out' *"wealth"* both visually and tactilely. In a similar way to the image of the morning rose this one captures that brief moment in which the promise and fulfilment of beauty are finely balanced, just before the bud opens.

In these images of natural, transient beauty all the reader's senses are brought into play to create a characteristic synthesis of concreteness and universality, which has been shown to exist wherever Keats visualises life's actual wealth and the potential arising from it.[91] In the preceding odes this condition is set aside somewhat from life as the poet experiences it. In **Ode on Melancholy** Keats shows that beauty exists and can be experienced as a reality in natural life.

ODE ON MELANCHOLY

Moving away from strictly external nature the poet now focuses on an outburst of emotion. *"Rich anger"* expresses the explosive natural energies residing in the uncontained and uncurtailed human emotions and reminds one of Keats' famous comment: *"though a quarrel in the street is a thing to be hated, the energies displayed in it are fine; the commonest Man shows a grace in his quarrel"*.[92]

The speed with which the outburst is expected to blow over is subtly suggested in *"mistress"*. In its suddenness and brevity it might be compared to the April shower. The lover is advised to feast on the unparalleled beauty of his mistress' eyes, heightened by the energy of her anger. Once more the momentary and the sense of endless potential meet - here in the briefness of the anger and in the energy and beauty which it releases. *"Deep, deep"* points towards *"peerless"* and evokes depth of feeling as well as the intensity required to apprehend beauty. Through melancholy we experience this beauty with fully stimulated powers, and melancholy in its turn is produced by such experience. Melancholy and the full appreciation of natural beauty go hand in hand.

The unifying factor in the images of stanza II, in diametrical contrast to stanza I, is their exclusive reference to the beauty of natural process, a beauty that may be appreciated by anybody with awakened senses. Melancholy is to be nourished on life, not death. It heightens the awareness of life's vital dynamism. The transient peak, the brevity of intense sensory awareness, and the universal contained in a fleeting moment of beauty are aspects inherent in all the individual images of stanza II. Life is the source of and the key to melancholy.

A number of critics take no heed of the qualitatively new type of melancholy put forward in the antithesis of stanza II. Bloom, for example, writes:

The enduring color of fresh life is only a grave color, and so your sorrow can also be glutted on the loveliness of such supposedly non-sorrowful emblems as a morning rose (...)[93]

The critic fails to recognise that melancholy is to be cultivated at the high point of sensuous living.

Leavis, too, makes little effort to distinguish the differing quality of the two concepts of melancholy confronting each other in the thesis and antithesis:

> *Keats's melancholy attracts no doubt both the 'weeping' and the 'cloud' quite naturally; but it is not, as the poem conveys it, at all like the sudden rain that refreshes the flowers. For the 'pale forehead' of the addict it has no such virtue.*[94]

But this is exactly Keats' point. He rejects the addict's pose of stanza I. He knows that melancholy does not revive and refresh someone who seeks it in darkness and death. It only functions in this way when it is experienced spontaneously and cultivated on life's finest moments. The addict's pose prevents the experience of true melancholy.

III

What is expressed in the language of images in stanza II is generalised in stanza III:

> *She dwells with Beauty - Beauty that must die;*
> *And Joy, whose hand is ever at his lips*
> *Bidding adieu; and aching Pleasure nigh,*
> *Turning to Poison while the bee-mouth sips:*

The meaning of "*She*" has been discussed widely. Some critics see it as referring to the mistress while others insist that melancholy is meant. The problem ought to be looked at in the light of the ode as a whole. Up to this point there has been a thesis and an antithesis. One would expect the third and final stanza to arrive at a conclusion. And since melancholy is the subject of the poem it seems likely that this will also be the theme of the conluding stanza.[95]

The three introductory images of stanza III (lines 1 - 4) generalise the insights of stanza II. But not all are at the same level of generalisation. There is a progression in sensuousness and precision which culminates in the image of *"aching Pleasure"*. The first two images refer to stanza II's message that melancholy and the intense experience of beauty's climax - beauty that must die - coexist and condition one another.

The third image not merely defines the culmination, which is already expressed in *"aching Pleasure"*, but like the image of the *"rainbow of the salt sand-wave"* it traces the movement from this culmination to its turning to dust. This process is compared to the time a bee takes to sip nectar from a flower, demonstrating at the same time the sensuous pleasure of *"tasting"* the culmination.

The final section intially returns to a more abstract level of generalisation:

Ay, in the very temple of delight
Veil'd Melancholy has her sovran shrine,
Though seen of none save him whose strenuous tongue
Can burst Joy's grape against his palate fine;
His soul shall taste the sadness of her might,
And be among her cloudy trophies hung.

The image of Melancholy's shrine in the temple of delight polemically refers back to the worship of melancholy in stanza I. *"Veil'd Melancholy"* and *"sovran shrine"* seem formidable, as the goddess Moneta does in **The Fall of Hyperion**. Another similarity between the two goddesses is that only those can cross the threshold of their realms who are prepared to enter fully into life. While in **The Fall of Hyperion** it is those

to whom the miseries if the world
Are misery, and will not let them rest

it is he

whose strenuous tongue
Can burst Joy's grape against his palate fine

in **Ode on Melancholy**. Life's experience must be pushed to its utmost limits in defiance of what follows. Otherwise the culmination may never be experienced and one will go through life without ever grasping its essence. **Fullest possible sensuous perception of beauty at its most intense thus becomes an important criterion for a person's readiness to confront life.** The prize is an insight into life's totality and dynamic potential, its price the momentary loss of beauty after intense experience of it. Living to the full requires strength and courage. This is indicated in the image of *"Joy's grape"*. Melancholy can only be seen by those who are prepared to face life's intensity with all it entails. At the same time melancholy heightens this experience. It is a **necessary concomitant** of pleasure-in-life and excludes **weltschmerz**.

In the image of *"Joy's grape"* the reader is confronted with the alternative of bursting the grape or preserving it. This is in fact the choice between responding appropriately to the grape, or not. The supreme enjoyment of the grape lies in its eating, which entails its disappearance. It can only be preserved if it is appreciated purely tactilely. This image recalls the *"ruby grape of Proserpine"*. Attractive though the latter is, it can never be sensuously enjoyed as this grape can.

Symbolically, it is the soul that *"tastes"* the *"sadness of her might"*. The reader is reminded that melancholy is a state of the soul. Furthermore the verb makes clear that the soul experiences melancholy naturally, not as an artificial construct of the intellect.

Experiencing melancholy remains ambivalent to the end. Its tribute is sadness. Therefore the soul that is affected by melancholy is both victor and victim.

In **Ode on Melancholy** the question of the possible superiority of a beauty independent of life no longer arises. It is from life alone that all the images, pointing to where true melancholy is to be found, are taken. Hence Leavis' conclusion that the ode

> *(...) represents one of the most obviously decadent developments of Beauty-addiction*[96]

seems unacceptable. Basing himself on the results of his own foregoing struggles, Keats now unconditionally affirms the supremacy of life's beauty. The image of *"Joy's grape"* clearly expresses the conviction that life must be met in a way appropriate to life if human beings want to live in a way proper to their own **human** nature. Part of this is the mobilisation of all human senses in the appropriation of reality. The reader is obliged to employ all 'mental senses' in imaginatively realising the images and in so doing 'experiences' the reward of courage. In this way our readiness to welcome life in all its contradictory intensity is finely cultivated. Keats' view of life, as it emerges in this ode, is the opposite of tragic; it is a celebration of the sensuous wealth of this world, a yes to reality.

For this reason it is also difficult to agree with Garrod's opinion:

The **Grecian Urn** *we may suppose to have been written in a mood of strong revulsion from the thesis of* **Melancholy**.[97]

All the foregoing suggests that **Ode on Melancholy** was written after and in answer to the questions raised and the struggles waged in **Ode to a Nightingale** and **Ode on a Grecian Urn**.

In a similar way to **Ode on a Grecian Urn**, **Ode on Melancholy** deals with general problems of human existence. It is, historically speaking, not quite as specific as **Ode to a Nightingale**. The organic interpenetration of happiness and sadness is seen as an essential creative element in existence. This is celebrated in **Ode on Melancholy**. (Compare also **Welcome Joy and Welcome Sorrow**.) Eternal, unchanging joy and beauty deny culmination (cf. **Ode on a Grecian Urn**). They are abstractions alien to life, because they cannot be directly experienced. True beauty exists only in the totality and abundance of reality, in its process, which can be captured and 'preserved' in the images of poetry. Melancholy stimulates a constructive and truly appropriate attitude to life. It is an integral part of life, a natural condition that is welcome because it revives and stimulates insight into the dialectics of human existence.

TO AUTUMN

The poetry of earth is never dead

As Keats left no clear indication in his letters or elsewhere concerning the sequence in which the spring odes were written such an order can only be established hypothetically on the basis of evidence in the poems themselves. I have attempted in the foregoing chapters to present and substantiate my own view. There can be little doubt, however, that **To Autumn** was the last of the odes to be written, after a break of several months.

Strictly speaking, **To Autumn** should not automatically be incorporated into the body of odes for two reasons. First, unlike the other poems its title does not indicate that Keats considered this an ode. Secondly, the 11-line stanza form differs from the previously employed 10-line form (excepting **Ode to Psyche**). If **To Autumn** is to be regarded as an integral part of the ode sequence this must be justified on the basis of a continuity of concern.

The concern has been twofold. One underlying theme of all the odes has been the nature of beauty, the other the relationship between art, the artist and life. One aspect of the latter theme was a discussion of the different possibilities of visual art and poetry. Poetry is eventually given preference (cf. stanza IV of **Ode on a Grecian Urn** and indirectly in the poetic images of stanza II, **Ode on Melancholy**) because it can capture and preserve more truly life's living beauty in its process.

The analysis of **To Autumn** must show in what way these themes are developed and if they confirm the position taken in **Ode on Melancholy**.

The opening address

Season of mists and mellow fruitfulness,
Close bosom-friend of the maturing sun;

evokes a multisensory image of autumn. The closeness of the friendship between autumn and the *"maturing sun"* indicates their inseparability, that the maturing sun is another aspect of autumn. Indeed, *"mellow fruitfulness"* can only arise from the sun's maturing. At the same time, of course, the sun itself is maturing and this steeps the entire image in the warmth and glow of a late summer afternoon.

Their cooperation deepens the active association of the sun and the season:

> *Conspiring with him how to load and bless*
> *With fruit the vines that round the thatch-eves run;*
> *To bend with apples the moss'd cottage-trees,*
> *And fill all fruit with ripeness to the core;*

Contradictory features of autumn are shown in their unity. The feeling of completion and yet of unceasing fertility and ripening are subtly conveyed, for example, through the varied use of end-stopped and run-on lines. This conflict in the images is paralleled by another unity of opposites: the fusion of fixity and movement, of solidity and process, of autumn as a season with eternal features and their particularisation in this specific autumn. The particularisation is achieved by the multisensory build-up of the images which gives them a specific taste and touch despite the high level of generalisation.

"Moss'd cottage-trees" is an example of this. The image is particularised through the sense of touching the trees and the very slight movement indicated in *"To bend"* which contrasts with *"run"* in the previous image, thus developing the sense of all-inclusiveness which was introduced with the contrast *"mists"* and *"maturing sun"*. The fixity and age of the trees, on the other hand, is expressed in the past participle form (*"moss'd"*)[98] as well as the use of the end-stopped line. On another level this fusion of the general and the specific is conveyed in the contrast between the *"cottage-trees"* and the mobile vines. Both the trees and the vines are depicted growing together with the cottage, thus implying complete harmony between nature and human beings.

With *"And fill all fruit with ripeness to the core"* the poet's attention shifts from the quantitive to the qualitative aspect of fertility. Ripeness penetrates from the outside - with the help of the sun - to the centre, or *"core"*. *"Core"* refers not only to the seed from which the fruit grew but also to that of the future generation, thus suggesting coming maturity.

> *To swell the gourd, and plump the hazel shells*
> *With a sweet kernel*

combines the ripening core with the fruit's expanding size. The images renew the idea of nature's pregnancy, which is hinted at in the first half of the stanza (*"load and bless/ With fruit"*). Juxtaposing two 'earth-products' of the most diverging types, tastes and sizes (gourd and hazel nuts), putting the one in the singular and the other in the plural, Keats, with his characteristic drive towards universality, enlarges upon the preceding contrasting pairs and thus conveys the all-round way in which nature is affected by autumn's conspiracy with the sun.

The movement of ripening is extensively developed in the following lines:

> *to set budding more,*
> *And still more, later flowers for the bees,*
> *Until they think warm days will never cease,*
> *For Summer has o'er-brimm'd their clammy cells.*

The idea of process conveyed in *"set budding"* is deepened in the run-on line but halted momentarily by the comma, thus renewing the feeling of movement arrested, of the season's simultaneous progress and completion in every moment. The object - *"flowers"* - is withheld twice, through *"And still more"* and *"later"*, both indicating process in themselves. Abundance of fruit is not just produced once, but is a continuous overflow of plenty, comparable to Proserpine's horn.[99] *"Later"*, while it suggests new buds opening, implies, however, that this seemingly endless maturing and fertility must come to an end.

While the previous images depicted the ripening of fruit cultivated by and for humans, this one shows the liaison between the vegetable and the animal parts of nature (the bees), and the connection with human cultivation and consumption is less direct. Thus, human beings are never very far from the centre of any of these images where life is in its true domain, where there exists a cohesion between all parts of natural life, which potentially includes the human community.

With this concluding image of the stanza the theme of duration and super-abundance reaches its climax.

II

From a late summer **anticipation** (*"Conspiring with him how to"*) of the plentiful outcome of the fertile alliance between autumn and the sun, concluding with the merest hint of winter, in the bees-image, stanza II moves into the middle of the harvest. Now the essential tie between nature and humanity emerges more clearly defined than in the opening stanza. This tie is epitomised in the autumn figure. Autumn and the peasant merge and there is a mutual enrichment. Through the depiction of autumn engaged in various kinds of farm work the peasant is raised to the level of a mythological figure and autumn assumes human contours. This synthesis is at the heart of all the stanza's images:

> *Who hath not seen thee oft amid thy store?*
> *Sometimes whoever seeks abroad may find*
> *Thee sitting careless on a granary floor,*
> *Thy hair soft-lifted by the winnowing wind;*

The peasant-autumn figure lives, through Keatsian fusion of high stylisation and overwhelming sensuous specificity, as convincingly, in its different mode, as the peasant figures do in Burns or Clare. Keats' highly-wrought image sets out to capture the essence of autumn. It is not his intention to depict scenes from village life as it is, but to show the harmony and cohesion that exists in nature as an exemplary paradigm-image for the proper mode of existence for all life. Hence the peasant figure is fused with autumn and becomes its personification.

Although the opening question implies that almost everybody has observed autumnal scenes like these, *"seeks abroad"* suggests a certain amount of necessary effort. *"Thee"* introduces the vivid portrait of humanised autumn. The image of the seated figure radiates tranquility and harmony. Behind its freedom from cares we imagine a plentiful harvest. The impression of stillness is both intensified and broken by the *"winnowing wind"*. The caress of *"soft-lifted"* deepens the sense of nature's internal harmony and the endless tenderness possible in her relations with humanity. The concentration of stressed syllables makes us read the words more slowly[100], that is more caressingly. The idea of a breeze entering is supported by the double /ft/ sound.

A similar use of sound is made in *"wínnòwìng wínd"*, while the rhythm is now quickened by a concentration of unstressed syllables between the stresses. The visual image conjured up by *"winnowing"* is of the ageing figure's hair, rather thin and sparse, being winnowed away by the wind of passing time. Thus the wind is simultaneously high autumn (still warm) and the first breath of the year's movement towards a change of season.

The image of autumn personified continues:

> *Or on a half-reap'd furrow sound asleep,*
> *Drows'd with the fume of poppies, while thy hook*
> *Spares the next swath and all its twined flowers:*

Again, the picture is one of complete tranquility. Sleep halts the progressing harvest midway. This moment of arrested movement becomes a reality in the poem through the insertion *"Drows'd with the fume of poppies"*, which appears to deepen the sleep and separates the harvester from the continuation of his half-finished work. The thought of interrupted activity which was introduced in *"half-reap'd furrow"* is taken up again in *"while thy hook/ Spares"*. This movement-laden 'stasis', so characteristic of Keats, charges the image with latent dynamism.

The sense of teeming abundance conveyed in *"swath"* and *"twined"* suggests the same wholeness of nature found in the second stanza of **Ode on Melancholy.** For the swath and the intertwining wild flowers, the harvester is the Great Reaper who puts an end to their life. There is a kind of culmination here indicated in the packed and colour-drenched imagery, and a simultaneous sense of imminent loss. Looking back to **Ode on Melancholy** one could say, that for this part of nature, autumn is that culmination of beauty, resulting, necessarily, in a dying that is part and condition of nature's greater life.

What seemed like unending growth has drawn to a close. The beauty of autumn's maturing cannot be separated from its harvesting.

However, **To Autumn** does not merely reproduce on a larger scale the beauty concept which lies at the heart of **Ode on Melancholy**. It develops this. In **Ode on Melancholy** to enjoy life's beauty to the full requires readiness to see it turn to dust. In **To Autumn** this sense of loss, though still there, is far less pronounced. Beauty is preserved for use and therefore more than a source of melancholy. The emphasis here lies on process and continuity.

The interconnection of fixity and movement in the ode's images is a product of the fusion of life and art: the movement of natural life is captured by the powers of art and yet it is not fully 'frozen', but goes on. Verse permits the movement to continue from the smallest unit of its imagery to the largest. The slight movement (or anticipated movement) within the individual images indicates the season's almost imperceptible progress. This progress takes larger strides in the sequence of images inside each stanza, and beyond that in the succession of the stanzas. This quality of capturing life's dynamic process through poetry demonstrates the marriage of life and art as proposed in **Ode on a Grecian Urn**, their proper and mutually enrichening relationship.

In accordance with the season's process, the next image implies that the field is completely harvested:

And sometimes like a gleaner thou dost keep
Steady thy laden head across a brook;

The figure now moves, becomes active. Many critics[101] have commented on Keats' magnificent artistry in making felt the gleaner's balancing across the brook. This is achieved by the sequence of two stresses, one at the end of one line and the other at the beginning of the next: *"keép/ Stéadÿ"*, giving the impression of careful stepping.

The image of the gleaner reminds one of a similar scene in Clare's *"October"* in **The Shepherd's Calendar:**

> *The milkmaid stepping with a timid look,*
> *From stone to stone, across the brimming brook;*
>
> (lines 13-14)

Compared to Clare, Keats gives the impression of slower balancing due to the heaviness of the load.

The concluding lines of the stanza introduce an activity that clearly points to the preparation for winter, one of the last tasks before the cold weather sets in:

> *Or by a cyder-press, with patient look,*
> *Thou watchest the last oozings hours by hours.*

In a similar way to the image of the *"later flowers"* and the bees in stanza I the movement indicates that of the season, only now the progression of time comes much closer to winter. The drawing to a close of the season is captured virtually by the minute as the *"last oozings"* emerge from the press. Again art, the poetic image, captures and heightens our feeling for autumn's contradictory features in their unity of seemingly never-ending and ending, of irresistable movement and its momentary arrestation.

III

The day and the season, drawing to a close, go out in a final blaze of beauty, in the kindly glow of the autumn sun setting on the harvested fields. Autumn and the sun have fulfilled their promise. Autumn has yielded and harvested the year's fruit and is now ready for winter. The stanza's theme is autumn's farewell symphony.

> *Where are the songs of Spring? Ay, where are they?*
> *Think not of them, thou hast thy music too, -*

TO AUTUMN

> *While barred clouds bloom the soft-dying day,*
> *And touch the stubble-plains with rosy hue;*

The stanza opens with an expansion of vision, contrasting with the close-ups preceding it. The prospect reaches to the very horizon and suggests infinity. As so often Keats uses oxymoron to capture the dialectics of change: the dying is a new birth of the process that culminates in autumn. After this image the heavy colour and warmth which distinguished stanzas I and II are quietly drained from the scene, making a contrast to the preceding stanzas as water-colour would to oil painting. There is a rarification of the previous sensuous universality which corresponds to the crispness of the autumn air and is a part of the poem's movement. In this way the waning into late autumn and evening is sensuously 'mimed'.

With evening, too, aural sense-perception comes to the fore. The music begins:

> *Then in a wailful choir the small gnats mourn*
> *Among the river sallows, borne aloft*
> *Or sinking as the light wind lives or dies;*
> *And full-grown lambs loud bleat from hilly bourn;*
> *Hedge-crickets sing; and now with treble soft*
> *The red-breast whistles from a garden-croft;*
> *And gathering swallows twitter in the skies.*

It is *"Then"*, at the close of autumn, that its specific music becomes audible. The voices that make up the symphony are all characteristic of late autumn and suggest impending winter. The gnats start up their wailing with the dusk, mourning the end of autumn and their own imminent death. In this extended image the ear is joined by eye and the sense of movement to create a high degree of sensuously complex immediacy. This image demonstrates that the modification of the sensory in correspondance with the time of day and year **creates a different kind of beauty that deepens and overcomes** the sadness of the gnats. The changing season brings with it a changing quality of beauty which hints at Keats' line *"The poetry of earth is never dead"*. **Beauty, then, is not something static, only present in the state of fulfilment. There is no diminution here. Winter will bring a beauty of its own.**

The uninterrupted sequence of stresses in *"smáll gnáts móurn"*, *"líght wínd líves"* and *"fúll-grówn lámbs loúd bleát"* are built-in moments of retardation in the line's rhythmic movement, clinging, as it were, to each moment as it passes in the direction of winter. These changes of pace subtly correspond to certain emotional emphases - the elegiac mood brought about by the mourning gnats, to types of sustained physical movement - the rising and falling of gnat-clouds on the wind, and to kinds of sound - the bleating of the sheep.

In using the phrase *"full-grown lambs"* instead of 'sheep' Keats describes the animal world as he did the world of vegetation previously: these are the ripened fruit of the year, bearing within themselves the seed of the coming year. In this image too the idea of winter is absent. For the sheep it is only the end of their lamb-time, the fulfilment of one stage of their development.

The nearer *"hedge-crickets"* join in the symphony with their particular 'instrument'. This movement inwards corresponds to that of humans in the change of the season from autumn to winter. The closing-in is continued in the image of the red-breast now settled and awaiting winter in the cottage garden. This hints once more at the integration of the human community into the overall picture of autumnal nature.

Despite the fact that all the animals in fact 'sing' simultaneously, the order in which they are brought into the visual and acoustic image traces the season's ever closer approach to winter. Note how the redbreast's voice is introduced relatively late, like a single flute into a choric harmony.

The poem ends with a dramatic leap out of the enclosed intimacy of the garden back into the immensity of the autumnal skies. The swallows, like the sheep and the redbreast, will not die, but live through the winter. Like the redbreast, the swallows are not plaintive, but prepare for winter. Both the swallows and the redbreast are, in this context, harbingers of winter. The contrast between the two types of bird - their different preparations for winter, their opposite locations, and their contrasting numbers - hint at a universality which is extended in the swallows' double nature: when they return they will be the heralds of spring.

In *"gathering"* motion is fused with the final - momentary - suspension of movement this autumn and in this ode. The anticipated flight will be followed by winter. But the beauty of nature is indestructible. Its changing beauty, being taken up to the very threshold of winter, implies that it will continue beyond this. Here there is no turning to poison or ashes. **Natural** dying after fulfilment is an organic part of beauty (cf. the image of the violets in stanza V of **Ode to a Nightingale**). Wasting away without fulfilment under certain social conditions and death as an escape from life's challenge run counter to this concept of beauty which embraces all that is proper to life. It may even be possible to read **To Autumn** as a kind of allegory for Keats' own hopes and perspective-thoughts about harvesting his poetic 'grain' and the possibility of his dying thereafter, while continuing to live as an immortal poet. **To Autumn** thus puts into a more positive perspective the fears expressed in **When I have fears that I may cease to be**.

In contrast to Shelley's **Ode to the West Wind** (written October 1819!) there is no fear of winter expressed here, as it too will generate a beauty specific and appropriate to itself. Because Keats embraces **the whole of** the life of nature in its essential movement, this becomes an exemplary paradigm for **all** life. Human existence is no longer seen as something apart, but integrated into the whole. Keats shows that the beauty envisioned in stanza II of **Ode to a Nightingale** must not be sought in places detached from life. Life's beauty and its truth lie in the totality of natural process and the whole material world. Anything that runs counter to this truth is not beauty. Social conditions that tend to stifle people's ability to sensuously perceive beauty (cf. stanza III of **Ode to a Nightingale**) are thus alien to the beauty set forth here. Poetry preserves the vision of life's beauty and truth and helps the reader grasp it through its ability to fix the natural **process**. In partnership with life, art's ability to fix becomes an essential strength. This is what **To Autmn** is also about. The fusion between fixity and process suffuses this ode from the smallest building brick to the complete structure. It differs from the images depicting sculptured art in accordance with the different possibilities of verse and visual art. But they are united in the immense energy they radiate, preserved for us through Keats' poetry.

Poetry's function, in its devotion to the human soul, is to awaken the reader to the existence of beauty which is commensurate with human needs. The recognition of this truth demands an affirmative attitude to life and its changeability where it is not appropriate to human nature, i.e. where it diverges from truth. But the reverse is also valid: it is the affirmative attitude to life, substantiated in the spring odes, which enables us to grasp life's truth as beauty. In this way **To Autumn** is the culmination and finale of the spring odes.

The tendencies that emerged in my discussions of Keats-criticism in the preceding chapters apply by and large to the analyses of **To Autumn**.

Critics who recognise the element of fulfilment in this ode usually base their argument on the images of ripeness and maturity only, without integrating the aspects of process and 'death'. Thus Bate writes:

> *Moreover, it is life that can exist in much the same way at other times than autumn. Only two images are peculiar to the season - the "stubble-plains," and the "full-grown lambs." The mind is free to associate the wailful mourning of the gnats with a funeral dirge for the dying year, but the sound is no more confined to autumn alone than is the "soft-dying" of any day; and if the swallows are "gathering," they are not necessarily gathering for migration (...)* [102]

Bate is clearly trying to avoid the 'negative' aspects of process. By commenting on the stanza in such a way he ignores the specific synthesis of animal voices expressing a particular autumnal condition or activity. His interpretation, if true, would mean there is an inexplicable break in the poem's cohesion and movement. The theme of gathering is native to both the season and the ode, not only with regard to harvest, but also in the physical movement towards the warmth of the house in the last stanza. Thus the gathering of the swallows is a final variation on this theme. And not to notice this is to reveal insensitivity to the ode as a complete unit.

There is also the usual tendency among some critics to project their own 'modern' approach to human life as 'alienation' into Keats and his poem. Virgil Nemoianu maintains that

> *The first stanza pictures a high point of consummate natural-human symbiosis. (...)*
> *The second stanza describes the severing of this total union. Cutting and squeezing, knives and presses are symbols of the war between man and nature, which is at least part of any harvesting process. The last stanza is squarely set in a world where man's consciousness has broken away from nature; contemplation, not involvement, is the keynote here. The passage from cooperation to conflict and separation in relation to nature is closely linked to the movement from triumphant fertility to dry depletion and the wiry sounds of emptiness. (...) Such indications combined (...) suggest an image of an alienated human community, as opposed to some integrated and fertile one that must have preceded it./*[103]

We have here the development of, to say the least, eccentric conclusions out of some interesting individual insights - although in view of the orthodox historical pessimism of this kind of approach, perhaps they are not quite so eccentric after all. **To Autumn** expresses, down to the minutest detail, a message diametrically opposed to the one put forward by Nemoianu **et al**.

However, I would like to conclude this chapter by quoting critics who present the acceptance of process positively and without reservations, transferring the image of natural life to human existence. Perkins and Mayhead represent this kind of attitude. Thus Perkins writes:

> *(...) the objectivity of the last few lines suggests an acceptance which includes even the fact of death. But death here is (...) recognized as something in-woven in the course of things, the condition and price of all fulfillment, having like the spring and summer of life its own distinctive character or "music" which is also to be prized and relished. (...) Thus the symbol permits, and the poem as a whole expresses, an emotional reconciliation to the human experience of process.*[104]

Mayhead comments in a similar vein:

> *Here impermanence is accepted without the least trace of sadness, for the reason that Keats is able to see it as part of a larger and richer permanence. This greater permanence is the continuity of life itself, in which the impermanence of the individual human existence is one tiny aspect of a vast and deathless pattern.*[105]

CONCLUSIONS

There is, as we have seen, an underlying tendency in much of modern criticism of Keats' odes to interpret them as a turning away from life towards a realm of beauty incompatible with the ugliness of social existence.

A close analysis of the development of the two main, interrelated themes - the nature of beauty and the function of poetry - in the odes has led us to the conclusion that this widely held view is in fact untenable.

Ode to Psyche is about the poet's calling as priest of the human soul. Psyche is the *"power more strong in beauty"* who has taken over from the Olympians to *"reign/ In right thereof"*. The very fact that the human soul has become the proper god and that the poet feels compelled to be her priest indicates Keats' heightened awareness of the artist's social responsibility. As stanza IV indicates, this must be met by a new quality in poetry and in the concept of beauty, merging immediate sensuous delight with creative thinking.

In **Ode to a Nightingale** the lyrical subject initially feels that beauty exists only in the nightingale's realm - in nature and in the integrated village community depicted in stanza II. This beauty clashes with his life experience where it cannot unfold. But the two modes of existence are not irreconcilably opposed to one another. The nightingale's world contains nothing that is alien to human existence - on the contrary, its beauty ought properly to be all life's inherent principle.

Within this thematic framework Keats grapples with two kinds of poetry, both of which find expression in the ode. One of these is the medium of the ode as a whole. This expresses the reflections, the inner struggle of the lyrical subject. The other kind - spontaneously sensuous poetry 'detached' from the reflecting brain - is conceived as the vehicle of escape from the concsiousness of reality. In that this, through the very nature of Keats' poetic approach, heightens the sensuous awareness of the beauty of the natural world, it defeats its own purpose by leading the lyrical subject back into the reality from which he seeks to escape.

The function of visual art and its relationship to poetry and life is uppermost in **Ode on a Grecian Urn**. Closely connected with this is a discussion of sculptured art's beauty and that of life. A supremacy of visual art over life is initially based on the former's ability to fix and eternalise moments of highest vitality and creativity. This opening thesis of the ode cannot be upheld. It emerges that sculptured art lacks life's pulse, its movement through contradiction. As part of the experience of life's beauty, it sharpens one's awareness of life's dynamism, but it cannot be a substitute for it. It is in life that the ultimate source of beauty must be sought.

The implicit comparison between sculpture and verse in this ode reveals the poet's growing certainty that his own art form is better suited to embody life's process.

Art's possibilities are not discussed directly in **Ode on Melancholy**. But some of the images **demonstrate** the ability of verse to capture and preserve dynamic process.

In this ode the true culmination of beauty is shown to exist in natural life. Its highest intensity cannot be separated from its turning to ashes. And here, in the dialectics of natural life, true melancholy is found if one is prepared to face life in its complexity and contradiction.

The themes of beauty and the function and possibility of poetry are brought to their conclusion in **To Autumn**. What is only hinted at in **Ode on a Grecian Urn** and **Ode on Melancholy** takes on clearer contours here: truth lies in natural life's process and universality, in its material totality and total materiality. It is here that one must search for its specific, dynamic beauty. In this sense truth and beauty are one. They are that which is proper to life in its development, commensurate with human needs. Truth and beauty **exist** in natural life, but in society they are being stifled. The beauty made manifest in nature ought also to be inherent to human living. The life of nature is hence a paradigm for human life, pointing to the positive potential in social actuality, to the embryo within it of that better world which is commensurate with humanity.

In spite of his great admiration for visual art it emerges from **To Autumn** that Keats sees poetry as the most fully adequate partner of life.

CONCLUSIONS

Poetry's ability to preserve for us and heighten our experience of life's process is **celebrated** in this final ode. It embodies the anticipated synthesis of immediate sensuous poetry with creative thought. Thus the odes and above all **To Autumn** are Keats' strategic justification of his own sense of calling, his defence of poetry as the most appropriate way of worshipping the human soul.

It was Bernard Shaw who first noted a similarity between Keats and Marx:

> *(...) Keats achieved the very curious feat of writing one poem of which it may be said that if Karl Marx can be imagined as writing a poem instead of a treatise on Capital, he would have written **Isabella** (...) it contains all the Factory Commission Reports that Marx read, and that Keats did not read because they were not yet written at his time.*[106]

Our analysis has tended to underline the connection between the two, if from a somewhat different angle. There is a definite parallel between Keats' vision of the whole person, able to make fullest use of the physical and mental senses in appropriating the world and its beauty, and the young Marx' thinking on human sensibility expounded in the Economic and Philosophic Manuscripts of 1844.

Marx notes two conflicting tendencies in the development of the human senses. On the one hand the *"**forming** of the five senses is a labour of the entire history of the world down to the present."*[107] On the other hand, under the conditions of private property, in *"place of all these physical and mental senses there has come the sheer estrangement of all these senses - the sense of **having**. The human being had to be reduced to this absolute poverty in order that he might yield his inner wealth to the outer world."* [108] The resolution of this conflict, Marx argues, takes place with the disappearance of private property. This revolution is seen as *"the **genuine** resolution of the conflict between man and nature (...)"*[109].

Keats too sees the full and active unfolding of the human senses in a way appropriate to them as the determining factor in the kind of society to be aimed at. Like Marx, Keats does **not** conceive of that better world as something quite detached from things as they are. The future is quarried out of actuality, exists in embryo within it. This, for Keats, is the beauty that is truth.

How is it that Marx and Keats could have come to such similar convictions? One reason perhaps lies in the fact that both were writing in the epoch during which the effects of the Industrial Revolution were making themselves felt. If one agrees with Marx that the *"forming of the five senses is a labour of the entire history of the world down to the present"* then the Industrial Revolution must clearly have opened up a completely new realm for the potential and real development of the human senses. Indeed, this would seem to be Marx' view when he comments

> *It will be seen how the history of **industry** and the established objective existence of industry are the **open** book of **man's** essential powers, the exposure to the senses of human psychology.*[110]

While Keats did not reflect on the new era in latent human sensuousness as Marx does here, it seems significant that he came, as a poet, both to possess and express such a heightened sensuous awareness at just this point in history - and with him others like Burns and Blake. Thus, while not denying that Keats' poetic programme is to a certain extent a revulsion against capitalist industrialisation, we are suggesting that the new sensuous quality of this poetry could perhaps only have been achieved **on the positive basis** of the Industrial Revolution as the *"open book"* of humanity's sensuous being.

BIBLIOGRAPHY

1. Kenneth Allott, *John Keats. A Reassessment*, Liverpool, 1969.
2. W. J. Bate (ed.), *Keats. A Collection of Critical Essays*, New Jersey, 1964.
3. Walter Jackson Bate, *John Keats*, London / Melbourne / Toronto, 1967.
4. Cleanth Brooks, *The Well-Wrought Urn*, London, 1968.
5. Robert Burton, *The Anatomy of Melancholy*, London, 1893.
6. R. A. Foakes (ed.) *Romantic Criticism 1800 - 1850*, London, 1972.
7. Richard Harter Fogle, *The Romantic Pleasure*, Athens, 1974.
8. Boris Ford (ed.), *The Pelican Guide to English Literature*, vol. 5, Penguin Books, 1957.
9. G. S. Fraser (ed.), *John Keats: Odes*, Macmillan, 1971.
10. H. W. Garrod, *Keats*, Oxford, 1967.
11. H. W. Garrod (ed.), *Keats. Poetical Works*, Oxford, 1976.
12. Robert Gittings, *John Keats*, Boston / Toronto, 1968.
13. Robert Gittings (ed.), *The Odes of Keats & Their Earliest Known Manuscripts*, London, 1970.
14. Robert Gittings (ed.), *Letters of John Keats. A Selection*, Oxford, 1977.
15. Hegel, 'Vorrede', *Phänomenologie des Geistes*, Leipzig, 1949.
16. Graham Hough, *The Romantic Poets*, London, 1976.
17. F. R. Leavis, *Revaluation. Tradition & Development in English Poetry*, London, 1936.
18. Robin Mayhead, *John Keats*, Cambridge, 1967.
19. Karl Marx, *Economic and Philosophic Manuscripts of 1844*, Moscow, 1961.
20. Virgil Nemoianu, "The Dialectics of Movement in Keats's 'To Autumn'", in *PMLA*, 93 (1978).

21. Charles I. Patterson, "Passion and Permanence in Keats's *Ode on a Grecian Urn*", English Literary History, 1954.
22. David Perkins, *The Quest for Permanence. The Symbolism of Wordsworth, Shelley and Keats,* Cambridge Mass., 1965.
23. G. B. Shaw, *Memorial Essay on Keats.*
24. Stuart M. Sperry, *Keats the Poet,* Princeton, 1974.
25. Alan Tate, 'A reading of Keats', *On the Limits of Poetry,* New York, 1948.
26. Earl R. Wasserman, *The Finer Tone,* Baltimore, 1967.
27. Donald Wesling, 'The Dialectical Criticism of Poetry. An Instance from Keats', Mosaic, V, 2, 1972.

REFERENCES

1. Hegel, p. 28.
2. Fraser, p. 21.
3. Garrod, pp. 80-87.
4. cf. *Ode to a Nightingale*.
5. *Letters* , p. 37.
6. ibid.
7. Mayhead, p. 91.
8. ibid.
9. Allott, p. 84.
10. *Letters*, pp. 249-250.
11. ibid., p. 250.
12. *Hyperion*, II, lines 206-231.
13. e.g. Allot, pp. 88-89.
14. See for example his indirect comments on Godwin, *Letters*, pp. 164, 326.
15. Mayhead, p. 87.
16. Allot, p. 94.
17. Perkins, p. 225.
18. Allott, p. 94.
19. Perkins, p. 228.
20. Allott, p. 92.
21. cf. *The Excursion,* IV, lines 941-992.
22. Sperry, p. 255.
23. ibid., pp. 258-259.
24. Wasserman.
25. *Endymion*, I, line 295.
26. Wasserman, p. 16.
27. ibid., p. 181.
28. ibid., p. 183.
29. Garrod, pp. 106-107.

30. Hough, p. 174.
31. cf. also: *"The poem is not, as it is sometimes said, a contrast between his own despondency and the happiness of the bird."* ibid.
32. Wasserman, p. 191.
33. This is due to the stress-timed rhythm of the English language. The time interval between stresses is approximately the same, therefore successive stresses slow down speech comparatively. The more unstressed syllables there are between the stresses, the more rapidly they have to be pronounced.
34. Gittings, *John Keats*, p. 317.
35. Mayhead, p. 72.
36. Tate, in: Fraser, p. 155.
37. It is not uncommon for Keats to perceive evening tactilely: *"Now on the **moth-time** of that evening dim"* (*Lamia*, I, line 200).
38. Mayhead, pp. 72-73.
39. Bate, pp. 505-506.
40. Wasserman, p. 199.
41. ibid., p. 211.
42. *A Midsummer Night's Dream*, II, 1, lines 249 - 252.
43. *Endymion*, I, lines 30-33.
44. Wasserman, p. 211.
45. The fact that the culmination takes place at midnight might be suggested by the meeting of the old and the new at this hour. cf. *Lamia*, I, line 27: *"There is a budding morrow in midnight"*.
46. Bate, *Keats*, p. 506.
47. cf. ref. 33.
48. Fogle, p. 38.
49. Wasserman, p. 218.
50. Wesling, p. 89.
51. *A Midsummer Night's Dream*, IV, i, line 150 ff.; V, 1, lines 432-436.
52. Wesling, p. 90.
53. Wasserman, p. 220.

REFERENCES

54. Bate, Mayhead, Wasserman.
55. e.g. Patterson.
56. cf. ref. 33.
57. cf. my introductory remarks to chapter II "Ode to a Nightingale" where the distinction is made between Keats and the poetical I, which is referred to as the 'lyrical subject'.
58. cf. *The Eve of St Agnes,* IV, lines 7-9:
   The carved angels, ever eager-eyed,
   Star'd, where upon their heads the cornice rests,
   With hair blown back, and wings put cross-wise on their
                                                                            breasts.
59. i.e. 'heaven's bourne', cf. p. 29.
60. Wasserman, p. 17.
61. Mayhead, p. 80.
62. Bate, p. 512.
63. cf. *On Seeing the Elgin Marbles* or a comment in a letter to George and Georgiana Keats about the prints of frescos in an Italian church: *"even finer to me than more accomplish'd works - as there was left so much room for Imagination." Letters,* p. 188.
64. Wasserman, p. 19.
65. ibid., p. 22.
66. ibid., p. 20.
67. Patterson, p. 210.
68. Represented here by Garrod.
69. Patterson, p. 209.
70. Ford (ed.), p. 236.
   cf. also Brooks, p. 129:
   "This third stanza represents (...) a recapitulation of earlier motifs (...) it represents a falling-off from the delicate but firm precision of the earlier stanzas. There is a tendency to linger over the scene sentimentally (...) Here (...) is to be found the blemish on the ode".
71. Walsh, *The Pelican Guide,* p. 236.

72. Wasserman, p. 30.
73. ibid., p. 37.
74. ibid.
75. ibid., pp. 40-41.
76. ibid., p. 19.
77. e.g. Walsh, p. 236.
78. Bate, p. 514.
79. T.S. Eliot, *Dante*, in: Fraser, p. 128.
80. Wasserman, p. 38.
81. Shelley, *A Defence of Poetry*, in: Foakes, p. 130.
82. Gittings, *Manuscripts*, p. 77.
83. See for example Letter to Bailey, 8 October 1817:
    Besides a long Poem is a test of Invention which I take to be the Polar Star of Poetry, as Fancy is the Sails, the Imagination the Rudder.
    (*Letters*, p. 27.)
84. Burton, p. 23.
85. Bloom, "The *Ode to Psyche* and the *Ode on Melancholy*", in: Bate, *Essays*, p. 99.
86. e.g. Mayhead, Allott; William Empson, "The ambiguity of 'Melancholy'", in: Fraser, p. 146-50.
87. At the time of writing I am not aware of any such analysis.
88. Garrod, p. 97.
89. Mayhead, p. 59.
90. Empson, in: Fraser, p. 147.
91. cf. *Ode to a Nightingale*.
92. *Letters*, p. 230.
93. Bloom, in: Bate, *Essays*, p. 100.
94. Leavis, p. 261.
95. Also the "mistress" image is clearly finished. It would be odd if one image out of a group, symbolising fit subjects for melancholy contemplation, should suddenly become the theme of the concluding verse.
96. Leavis, p. 260.
97. Garrod, p. 101.

REFERENCES

98. cf. my remarks on the use of the past participle to express arrested movement in *Ode to Psyche*, pp.12-13.
99. *cf. The Fall of Hyperion,* Canto I, lines *35-38:*
    Still was more plenty than the fabled horn
    Thrice emptied could pour forth, at banqueting
    For Proserpine return'd to her own fields
    Where the white heifers low.
100. cf. ref. 33.
101. e.g. Leavis, pp. 263-4.
102. Bate, p. 583.
103. Nemoianu, p. 211.
104. Perkins, p. 294.
105. Mayhead, p. 96.
106. Shaw.
107. Marx, p. 108.
108. ibid., p. 106.
109. ibid., p. 102.
110. ibid., p. 109.

**BREMER BEITRÄGE ZUR LITERATUR-
UND IDEOLOGIEGESCHICHTE**

herausgegeben von Thomas Metscher
und Dieter Herms

Band 1   Horst Rößler: Literatur und Arbeiterbewegung. Studien zur Literaturkritik und frühen Prosa des Chartismus. 1985.

Band 2   Priscilla Metscher: Republicanism and Socialism in Ireland. A Study in the Relationship of Politics and Ideology from the United Irishmen to James Connolly. 1986.

Band 3   Hagal Mengel: Sam Thompson and Modern Drama in Ulster. 1986.

Band 4   Gudrun Kauhl: Joseph Conrad: **The Secret Agent**. Text und zeitgeschichtlicher Kontext. 1986.

Band 5   Ingrid Kerkhoff: Poetiken und lyrischer Diskurs im Kontext gesellschaftlicher Dynamik. USA: >The Sixties <. 1988.

Band 6   Jennifer Farrell: "Keats - The Progress of the Odes. Unity and Utopia." 1988.

Lillie Jugurtha

Keats and Nature

New York, Berne, Frankfurt/M., 1985. 208 pp.
American University Studies: Series 4, English Language and Literature. Vol 18
ISBN 0-8204-0171-4 hardback sFr. 79.60

John Keats loved the out-of-doors-flowers, birds, water, fresh air, the sun, the moon, and the seasons. The sight, sound, or touch of nature could send him into emphatic responses. Keats never stopped responding to the sensations of nature. But his letters and poems record a movement from thinking of nature as scenery providing sensations to seeing nature as a source of truths about how and why men live. In *Keats and Nature*, Lillie Jugurtha analyzes this philosophical evolution which climaxed in a metaphysical view of nature (organicism). Jugurtha shows how this conception of nature allows one to read *Endymion, Hyperion,* and *The Fall of Hyperion* with new understanding and pleasure-- how it augments readings of minor poems, *The Eve of St. Agn0es, Lamia,* and the great odes.

Eva Volkmer-Burwitz

Tod und Transzendenz in der deutschen, englischen und amerikanischen Lyrik der Romantik und Spätromantik

Frankfurt/M., Bern, New York, Paris, 1987. XII, 437 S.
Europäische Hochschulschriften: Reihe 14, Angelsächsische Sprache und Literatur.
Bd. 177
ISBN 3-8204-1144-5 br./lam. sFr. 75,--

Die vorliegende Studie entwirft ein repräsentatives Bild der Todes- und Transzendenzauffassungen der romantischen und spätromantischen Lyrik, das sie am ikonographischen Repertoire von zwölf Dichtern aus drei Nationen aufzeigt. Ausgehend von der These, daß die Themenfelder Tod und Transzendenz im Zentrum romantischen Bewußtseins stehen und die philosophischen, theologischen und psychologischen Umbrüche dieser Epoche spiegeln, wurde versucht, den zeitgenössischen Prozeß der Säkularisierung am Wandel stofflicher und stilistischer Elemente nachzuweisen. Im Vordergrund der Untersuchung stehen die Dichter Hölderlin, Novalis, Heine und die Droste, Coleridge, Beddoes, Keats, E. Brontë, Longfellow, Poe, Whitman und E. Dickinson.

Verlag Peter Lang Frankfurt a.M. · Bern · New York · Paris
Auslieferung: Verlag Peter Lang AG, Jupiterstr. 15, CH-3000 Bern 15
Telefon (004131) 32 11 22, Telex pela ch 912 651

Charles De Paolo

Coleridge's Philosophy of Social Reform

New York, Berne, Frankfurt/M., Paris, 1987. XII, 273 pp.
American University Studies. Series 6, English Language and Literature. Vol. 58
ISBN 0-8204-0531-0　　　　　　　　　　　　　　　　　hardback sFr. 55.70

Reacting to empiricism, to idealism, and to conservative repression, Coleridge devised an eclectic social philosophy that combined Christianity, Kantian ethics, and Burkean conservatism. Evaluating the philosophical precursors and the contemporary context, De Paolo establishes the nature of Coleridge's reactions to these philosophies, determines the quality of his eclecticism, and considers the degree to which his social thought - which the author calls «conservative humanism» - informs and directs his opinions on such issues as child labor, national education, slave emancipation, and suffrage. De Paolo concludes that Coleridge's reformist work is a substantive and coherent statement on the social conditions of his times, one that earns him an important, and a hitherto unrecognized, position in the annals of social thought.

Brian Conniff

The Lyric and Modern Poetry
Olson, Creeley, Bunting

New York, Berne, Frankfurt/M., Paris, 1988. 218 pp.
American Studies: Series 4, English Language and Literature. Vol. 60
ISBN 0-8204-0533-7　　　　　　　　　　　　　　　　　hardback sFr. 54.80

The lyric poem has long been considered a «timeless» form, and rigid lyric conventions inform most modern poetry and criticism. Yet these conventions are not indicative of anything «essentially poetic»; rather, they hide our culture's fundamental contempt for poetry, our refusal to take it seriously. They can help even a great poet to dismiss his own work as unimportant, as in the case of W.H. Auden; or they can provide the focus for an all-out attack on the Western metaphysical tradition, as in the case of Charles Olson. Because poets like Olson, Robert Creeley, Basil Bunting, and Louis Zukofsky question the assumption most central to a lyric «genre», it is their writing that best exposes, and best resists, our deep distrust of poetry.

Verlag Peter Lang　Frankfurt a.M. · Bern · New York · Paris
Auslieferung: Verlag Peter Lang AG, Jupiterstr. 15, CH-3000 Bern 15
Telefon (004131) 32 11 22, Telex pela ch 912 651